AUTHORITY INFLUENCER MARKETING

Made Simple

GLOBAL
PUBLISHING
G R O U P

Global Publishing Group

Australia • New Zealand • Singapore • America • London

AUTHORITY INFLUENCER MARKETING

Made Simple

The No.1 Secret to stand out and dominate in any crowded market place, in any industry, any time

ANDREW CARTER

First Edition 2023

National Library of Australia
Cataloguing-in-Publication entry:

Authority Influencer Marketing Made Simple: the no.1 Secret to stand out and dominate in any crowded market place, in any industry, any time - Andrew Carter

1st ed.
ISBN: 978-1-925370-83-6 (pbk.)

 A catalogue record for this book is available from the National Library of Australia
NATIONAL LIBRARY OF AUSTRALIA

Published by Global Publishing Group
PO Box 258, Banyo, QLD 4014 Australia
Email admin@globalpublishinggroup.com.au

For further information about orders:
Phone: +61 7 3267 0747

Dedicated to all entrepreneurs, the business owners, the people who took the risk and created something special, often against the advice of those closest to them.

Considered outcasts by some, rebels by others and completely misunderstood by most, you are the people who actually make an ongoing difference in the world. You deserve to do well. This book was written to help you succeed greater than maybe even you thought was possible.

ACKNOWLEDGEMENTS

I must thank my incredible mentors who I have been fortunate enough to meet, work with and learn from. Each inspired me and helped me on my journey - Armand Moran, Darren Stephens, Mal Emery, Robert Kiyosaki and the late great Ted Nicholas. Thank you so very much for your wisdom, guidance and assistance.

A very special thanks to the incredible team at Global Publishing Group for making this book what it is.

Incredible FREE Bonus Offer just for purchasing this book

This is my way of rewarding the action takers. Many people have access to the same opportunities, yet few actually act on them. You have taken action by purchasing this book. Your business will succeed in a massive way if you continue to take action and apply what you learn in this book.

To encourage you to continue to take action at every stage I want you to have access to these incredibly helpful gifts **worth over $400 dollars**, all free of charge.

By using the QR code below (or visiting the website) you will get access to –

- A unique one off, live on stage, private video presentation by the man who wrote the forward for this book and applied the principles within to create a business paying him $1 million a year. In that 45 minutes he will break down step by step the exact process he uses and show you how you can do the same in your business.

- A digital download copy of my first two business books, written a long time ago but updated and still completely relevant today. One of those books was used as a coursebook and essential reading for the Advertising and Marketing course at the University of Canberra.

- Completely free (and obligation free) one on one introductory meeting (online or on phone) with five of the top professional organisations that can help you generate far more money in your business.

- Special, heavily discounted price for intensive live in person workshop to truly transform your business.

Just scan this QR code or go to
www.MarketingInfluencer.com.au

CONTENTS

FOREWORD

I was born in Wroclaw, Poland in 1976, and lived across the road from an old Church and Cemetery (a very Gothic Eastern European opening, I know, but stay with me here). As a child, I often pondered the fact that a cemetery is perhaps one of the unrealised richest places on earth because it is here that you will find all the hopes, dreams, and aspirations that were never fulfilled; the bestseller books that were never written, the block-buster movie scripts that were never completed, the number one song hits that were never sung, the life-changing inventions that were never completed and patented, and the thousands of business ventures and start-up companies that would never be. Not only is a cemetery a memorial to your body, but in millions of cases it's a memorial to dreams and ambitions that were never realised.

The saddest part of all of this is that the true reasons these talented entrepreneurs never succeeded is that they were simply too afraid of taking the first step (fear of success) or waited for the right time in their life to get started, which never came. Or they failed to learn the right system or methodology to use to complete what seemed like an insurmountable task at hand. Thus, most ideas die in the minds of entrepreneurs and business owners and never see the light of day.

I would have been one of those people, and for over 6 years I sat on a business concept that I knew would change lives... but I simply did not know how to get started. And you know how it is: you get caught up in the mundane routines and patterns of daily life, work, kids, marriage, gym, going out, and the years simply pass you by.

Millions of people around the world live out their lives in quiet desperation, each knowing that they were destined for a greater purpose, but eventually run out of time to implement their ideas.

I would have become one of those people, but for me, everything changed when I learned that nothing would happen with my concept until such time that I found:

A proven system or methodology to follow, and the right mentor or coach who could keep one (such as I) accountable.

Ten years ago, I found exactly that. A truly unique company showed me over one weekend the power of Authority and Influencer Marketing and how to apply that to my business concept, making my start up a stand out and successful business right from the start. My real estate business – Investors Prime Real Estate - skyrocketed, has made me a multi-millionaire, and has changed my and my family's lives, forever.

All this was possible only because I tapped into the proven system that creates a specific outcome and result. Not only that, I learned the number 1 secret of establishing yourself as an authority influencer in your own specific field; a number 1 Secret that was well-known to world-renowned authors, transformational coaches, business owners, and social influencers such as Robert Kiyosaki, Anthony Robbins, Brendan Burchard, Brian Tracy, Bob Proctor, and Jim Rohn, just to name a few. They all launched their businesses on the back of the authority each created in their chosen fields.

The reality is that no one knows or cares who you are or what your business is offering to the marketplace until you elevate yourself above the rest and set yourself up as an authority influencer in your desired field, just like I have.

Authority Influencer Marketing is the single most powerful tool available, bar none. Nothing else even comes close. It is what built my empire and my fortune so quickly. Although not well known, it is a simple concept and easy enough to execute if you have the right person to show you the way. In this book, Andrew will do just that.

This is not a long book because it doesn't need to be. Andrew covers the fundamentals and shows you how to easily create this incredibly effective system and use it to position yourself as the undisputed authority in your field, effectively making your competition irrelevant.

He will show you how to use this to maximum benefit and how to generate new income streams from it. He will also cover The Game Behind The Game, which can take your business to a level you probably never thought possible and create wealth faster than you ever imagined. That certainly was the case for me. This book will show those possibilities, the ones you're just not aware of, and will always miss out on, until you learn this.

The fastest way to success is by reading this book and applying these principles. They worked for me and they will work for others.

KONRAD BOBILAK
CEO – Investors Prime Real Estate
www.InvestorsPrime.com.au
www.KonradBobilak.com.au

INTRODUCTION

In many ways being in business can seem harder now than ever before. There is far more competition offline and online than at any other time. People are overexposed to far more advertising in a day than ever before. The aftereffects of COVID lockdowns, travel restrictions, staffing issues and disrupted supply chains, will be felt for a long time to come and the full fall out of all that will become evident many, many years later.

Working harder and longer isn't going to fix the issue but sadly it has become the norm for many business owners trying to survive. Many so called experts are offering services to get you noticed online; most are not successful. The few who are, only are until an algorithm or rule change by a search engine or social media operator occurs, then they're back to square one.

There has to be an easier way – and there is. A very simple solution, not known to many but used extensively by the incredibly successful – and that is what I will show you in this book. I must stress that this solution *is simple* because once it is revealed, you may automatically think you can't do it but you definitely can.

I will show you extremely easy, quick and cheap ways of achieving this goal with very little effort from you. I will show you plenty of real-life examples of average business owners and even hobbyists who have done it, and the successes that brought them.

More than that, I am going to show you how to create extra income from this and have you look at The Game Behind The Game - the ultimate business success from Authority Influencer Marketing that can bring you an entirely other level of wealth that you may never have expected.

Even if you choose not to follow that incredibly powerful step, Authority Influencer Marketing will position you as **THE** *Go-to Authority* and *Expert* in your field – and people want to deal with the expert, they will go out of their way to do so. People will pay more to deal with the expert. So follow the very simple steps in this book and be seen as that expert.

So how did I discover this and who am I to teach it to others?

I started my first business a long time ago, simply to help others. I always figured I'd make some money in it but that was never the driving force behind it. The specifics of what that business was are not as important as the how and the why it succeeded.

I had a lot of experience in a certain field and so I knew what products were best for people wanting to get into that. The problem was that all the good Australian manufacturers producing those products had gone out of business as cheap imports from China flooded the market. The Chinese products may have been cheap but they simply weren't suitable. When people approached me for a recommendation on what they should use, I became tired of having to tell them there simply wasn't anything suitable.

Why wasn't there anything suitable? I understood the Chinese manufacturers were just getting started in this area and they didn't understand what they needed to produce but I did - and I was in a position to do something about it. So I approached a manufacturer to produce exactly what the market required. Of course that was a long and arduous effort but it paid off and I then had something that exactly met the market need. It was far more expensive than my nearest competitor but far superior to what anyone else was selling.

To help educate potential customers about the product, so they knew why it was so much better and therefore more expensive, I put pictures of myself and my experience on my very basic website and provided generic information about the product, all available completely free.

Although it hadn't been my intention, what that did was establish my authority. It positioned me as the expert, without me ever saying I was. It meant that people all over the world found and came to my website for that information. Even though my products were only available in my country, more than 60% of traffic to my website everyday was from overseas.

Once perceived as the expert, my business life changed dramatically. As a small back yard, sole trader, I almost overnight started competing against the big boys, the major corporations, and my product became the second best seller nationally in its niche. The business grew and I employed staff.

I saw first hand the difference from being a struggling business trying to get noticed, to now having people pursuing me as a result of being positioned as the authority – and what a major impact that had on my profits and success. A business I had started to help people, was now making me wealthy. That's what happens when you position yourself as the go-to authority and can solve people's problems.

But all that was 16 years ago. A lot has changed online and offline in 16 years.

When I sold that business, other business owners who learnt about my success would approach me wanting to learn my secrets and how to apply it to their business. So although I never planned on becoming a business consultant and coach, by default that's what happened. Once again, I started a business to help other people.

I soon found there were a LOT of consultants out there, few with any real experience or even understanding but promoting themselves as experts anyway. So what was I going to do stand out from the charlatans? How was I going to be positioned as the go-to authority in this new field and become successful?

Luckily, I met a guy who had formulated what I am going to show you in this book and he had generated unbelievable (but completely verifiable) results from it. He wanted to teach it to a few people, basically as beta testers, and have them generate similar results to give him testimonial credibility to allow him to run a business teaching the process to others.

A dozen of us followed the steps you will read about and generated far greater results, far quicker than we could have without this incredibly powerful marketing tool. Some people generated phenomenal results from this and this alone.

People who never expected to ever be making 7 figures, now were. Others who had struggled in business discovered this was the missing piece of the puzzle that turned their business around almost instantly. I was amazed it worked as well as it did and couldn't believe that so few people knew about it. That successful system he created in 2007 has since taught thousands of people from all around the world and in all industries.

What I came to learn is that nearly all the biggest names in business around the world have used this same strategy themselves and that is what positioned them as the go-to authority and lead to their huge business success. You know of many of those people, you just don't know the tool they used – or how best to use it. This book covers that in detail.

This information is just too good. Business owners need to know it. I liked this marketing product and the results it generated so much that I bought the company! So, once again I find myself in a situation where I can dramatically help others and I now teach it to those who are serious about wanting to take their business to a whole new level.

By implementing this simple strategy, using the techniques covered in this book, you can literally make your business more successful than you had ever dreamed and generate so much more money than you ever expected.

CHAPTER ONE

What is Authority Influencer Marketing and what can it do for you?

> *The world does not reward ordinary people, so be seen as extraordinary.*
>
> **Andrew Carter**

CHAPTER ONE

What is Authority Influencer Marketing and what can it do for you?

Authority Influencer Marketing is the process by which you establish yourself as an expert in your industry. If people perceive you as a leader in a certain field, they are far more likely to use your products, services and advice, and in fact pay more for it.

Being successful in business relies on being able to sell, and to do that you need two things. You must be able to -

1. Gain attention
2. Build trust

You have to gain people's attention to let them know what you are selling. Far too many people think that just by opening a store, or by setting up a website, or placing an ad, or posting on social media or YouTube, that they will capture people's attention and make lots of sales. A long time ago you probably could. However, both the online and offline market are saturated. When you do any of those things today, you become another 'me too' business, another one of millions all doing the same thing. You need to do something that will really make you stand out from the crowd, something that will attract people's attention.

It is because of social media and the fact that we all carry smart phones, the amount of advertising we are exposed to each day online and offline, is conservatively estimated at 3,000 pieces – every day! Other studies have suggested it could be more than double that, which would have been inconceivable last century but certainly possible today.

As such, we are predisposed to simply tune out the constant bombardment of advertising we see each day. It just becomes white noise, something we just don't pay any attention to, meaning that 94% of all conventional advertising is completely wasted. Literally billions of dollars spent each year that doesn't even capture attention, yet alone create brand awareness or generate a sale.

The first thing Authority Influencer Marketing will do for you is gain attention. Used correctly, it not only attracts the correct client for you, it can actually repel those who aren't. Far too many businesses waste too much time dealing with people only to find they are just not the right type of client. Authority marketing allows you to *attract prospects, not rejects*. That might sound harsh but the reality is you deserve to earn more money for less work and that only comes from dealing with your ideal client.

Once you've attracted the ideal client, you then need to build trust. People are reluctant to purchase goods or services because of a lack of trust. We've all been burnt before and don't wish to be so again. So trust becomes the single biggest barrier to making a sale after you have gained a prospects attention. People like to buy from people they trust and building that trust can take a very long time.

Traditional marketing dictated that building trust should be done through a marketing or sales funnel, and you probably have one or at least tried one. It starts by advertising a free give away. That gets people into the top of your funnel, who provided their name and email address. You then have to follow up by giving loads of valuable information for free, before eventually offering for sale a low priced item. The reason being the customer still didn't quite fully trust you yet, so selling a low price (under $50) item wasn't seen as too confronting and the customer was likely to risk that small amount for the perceived benefit.

So how much free stuff did you have to give away before that first sale? The general rule of thumb was seven touch points. Meaning you needed to have provided meaningful information and free products to someone at least seven times in an effort to build some sort of credibility and trust with that person before asking for a sale of a small ticket item.

The problem with the funnel is twofold. It is a long and slow process that involves continually contacting the customer until they eventually purchase something or drop off your list completely. The other issue is it still required you to be noticed in the first place. What did you have to do to let people know that you were going to give a free PDF eBook or something? With everyone else trying to do the same thing, they all just become another 'me too' type business, basically another individual throwing a fishing line into already overfished waters, alongside literally millions of other fishermen doing the same.

When you position yourself as the expert or go-to authority in your niche you then stand out completely from all the other 'me too' businesses. You no longer have to hold your fishing rod hoping for a bite. The fish literally come to you and in big numbers.

If you don't believe you could be the expert or go-to authority in your business, just wait till you've read the next chapter. It states exactly why you can (and should be) and the rest of the book tells you how.

The need for this is far more important now than at any other time in history. Sure, we're all sick of hearing about COVID but the fact remains it has changed all our lives irrevocably. Many businesses have and will continue to fail as a result of it, so now is the best time to position yourself and your business above the others and have quality customers or clients come seek you out. You need your business to survive (and even thrive) in the tough economic times ahead, to really flourish when the economy gets stronger.

So I'm going to give you a strategy that has been proven over many, many years that will absolutely have far more customers wanting to buy your product or service. It doesn't matter where you are or what type of business you are in, online or offline, it will work for you. We've done this with literally thousands of people all around the world, in every type of industry and it's been proven time and again. **It actually reverses the dynamic of you having to chase customers or clients and instead has them chasing you.**

It doesn't matter whether you're in a retail, traditional bricks and mortar type business, or a service industry, or a completely online business, even if you're a purely online influencer. You can use this to get the right customers coming to you, and you can do it on a global scale.

So Authority Influencer Marketing is going to gain attention for you and build immediate high level trust and credibility quicker than anything else we've come across in a combined 60 plus years in marketing. It will generate massive FREE PR media online and in print, on radio, podcasts and on TV. It can also generate alternative income streams from other products you sell from this with very little work and also in what we call The Game Behind The Game, which many have found to be by far the largest benefit of implementing this strategy and one they simply couldn't have done without.

CHAPTER TWO

When a business gives a message we see it as advertising. When an individual authority does it, we see it as thought provoking or inspirational.

CHAPTER TWO

Why YOU are completely capable
of being seen as the Authority

The biggest resistance to creating Authority Influencer Marketing is the mindset of the business owner. Many simply don't think of themselves as the expert and so can't accept the idea of developing marketing that positions them as number one in their customers minds.

Note I wrote - *positions them as number one in their customers minds*, **not** - *positions them as number one.*

There is a subtle but considerable difference there. Later in this book I will cover the way in which to attract your audience, your ideal client, and repel the ones you don't want. Whatever shortfall in experience or knowledge you feel is currently holding you back from being seen as an expert, I will describe how to deal with that latter.

For now, you only need to know that **Authority and Status is** *Passion, Perception and Positioning.*

You clearly have the passion as you are taking the time to read this book and dramatically improve your business. This book will show you how to create the perception and the positioning through the ultimate Authority Influencer Marketing tool. Before I reveal what that is, I have to cover a few other key factors so that you can accept and apply what you will discover.

Often we are reluctant to try anything new, especially anything this life changing. Subconsciously at least, some fear creeps in. The subconscious likes things the way they are, as it knows how to deal with that. So when we introduce something new it tries to keep things the way they are by sending messages to your conscious brain which then tries to rationalise with 'logic' and tell you why you shouldn't be doing this new thing. I put the word logic in apostrophes because in times like that, logic isn't actually logical.

All too often we listen to and agree with that voice, after all it was providing good 'logical' reasons why we shouldn't do that new thing. However, that is the subconscious' 'self defence' mechanism which can create self sabotage, thereby restricting learning, growth and wealth creation.

Whenever you contemplate something new, give special awareness to the initial thoughts that come to mind as these defence mechanisms are easily identifiable. If you find yourself thinking –
I can't do that, or
That won't work for me, or
That's way too difficult, or
I just don't have the time to do that, or
I don't have the skill or knowhow,
then simply add the word "yet" at the end of that thought, to completely change your way of thinking and cause the subconscious to work against itself.

The subconscious is always active and can work on any issue until solved. If you say to it "I can't do that", then there is no need for it to work on that issue any longer. If however you said "I can't do that – yet", then the subconscious has to work on that until it comes up with a solution. This is why whenever we have a problem or a difficult decision to make, we are told to "sleep on it". The subconscious continues to work on the issue even when you are asleep, so when you wake up in the morning you think you've had an epiphany as the solution has just presented itself.

You'll be surprised just how powerful this simple mindset change can be in the long run. So your objections then turn into –
That won't work for me - yet
I just don't have the time to do that - yet
I don't have the skill or know how – yet

As far as it being way too difficult or you not having the time to do it, for reasons I will cover in this book, it's not and you will. It is exactly because most people think about this Authority Influencer Marketing tool being difficult and time consuming to create, that so few people do it. It is because people have those thoughts, that if you implement this strategy, it completely changes people's perception about you. They think that because you did this, then you MUST be the authority or go-to expert in that field, regardless of whether you actually think you are or not.

Again, **Celebrity, Authority and Status is *passion*, *perception* and *positioning***.
As long as you have passion, this book will help you create the positioning and the perception of being a celebrity or authority in your field or endeavour.

I'm going to overcome each and every one of your subconscious objections and show you easy, straight forward ways to **establish Authority Influencer Marketing in as little as half a day.**

Seriously! **I can show you how it can be done with little effort and even how you can have others do it for you.** So despite any initial objection you may find that comes up for you, you need to read through to the end of the book to see how simple this actually is and how completely effective it is in other people's lives, and know that it can be for you also.

CHAPTER THREE

Becoming the Authority

> *I have as much authority as the Pope. I just don't have as many people who believe it.*
>
> **George Carlin**

CHAPTER THREE

Becoming the Authority

No one has any problem viewing Tony Robbins, Dr John Gray, Russell Brunson, Deepak Chopra or those types of people as the experts or authority in their field. Everyone understands that those people make very large sums of money from professional speaking gigs, seminars and one on one coaching or group training sessions, because they're famous – right, the authority in their field?

Well, how did they become that authority in the first place?

They had to do something to become famous, to be perceived as the go-to authority or expert. So what was it?

It is the same thing that Jacqueline Coates, a single mother of two, did. Jacqueline left her corporate job because she wasn't passionate about it: her passion was art. So she started teaching people how to paint beautiful roses and blooms. That was her backyard business, however using our Authority Influencer Marketing strategy she took her backyard business globally, literally. She was so successful that she's bought houses in France and now takes high paying customers from Australia over to France, stay at her places and learn to do paintings in that European environment.

I cover many actual real life examples throughout the book (in much more detail) so that you realise that if those people can do it, you certainly can.

I spent a lot of money (well over $100,000) educating myself on marketing over many years, before and during my first business. It was that money I invested in my education that led to my success. Even though that was a huge sum of money at the time, it gave me the skills and the confidence to make back that entire six figure amount in my business, each month.

I made a point of learning from the best, both here and overseas. I found myself a mentor, as the fastest road to success is following in the footsteps of those who have already done it successfully. Mentors have proven systems in place for you to follow, allowing a much faster and easier path to success than they may have initially had. They can advise you of the pitfalls and problems before you ever encounter them so you can avoid the sorts of setbacks they experienced.

I've had several mentors over the years and I have met some of my mentors' mentors. They all had one thing in common, though I just couldn't see what it was at the time (possibly because I was star struck by their authority and celebrity status) until it was pointed out to me by one of them.

What made each of them an Authority? Believe it or not the answer is contained in the word, **Author**ity. To become an Authority, each of them first became an Author.

Initially that just seemed way too simple and I had trouble getting my head around it. "Surely you mean that you were the expert, attracted a huge following because of that and then wrote a book?"

"No, I wrote the book, was then perceived as the expert and attracted a huge following and then I created the products and services I sell".

Each Authority figure / guru I came across had followed the same path. Why did having a book create this perception about them? Because **being an author ranks in the top 10% of professions in terms of prestige.**

Authors are held in high esteem and are trusted, as is their message. A large part of that comes from people believing it is difficult to write a book and be published – and it is, unless you have a book like this to show you the simple tips, tricks and techniques to get it done quickly and easily, *even if you can't type or write!*

This was an absolute mind blowing revelation for me but now that my eyes were open I could see it everywhere and the answer was just so obvious.

A book is THE Number 1 builder of credibility and trust. There is nothing else like it.

Why? Well first and foremost authors are, and always have been, highly respected. Society has always looked at published authors as experts in their field – as THE Authority. When you are published, you automatically assume that mantle.

You do not have to state you are the expert or that you are credible. The book does that for you. The book acts as a third party, independent advocate of you and your business. So, you never have to go around saying, "I'm the expert or authority", merely being the author of the book on the subject, the perception is that you must be.

Note that all this refers to a physical book, a printed book. You can't gain any real credibility with an eBook and you're not really ever going to get noticed yet alone obtain celebrity or expert authority status with one.

Now let me clarify that. This is the one point that seems to cause the most confusion. So many people read or hear that statement and say – "What about so and so? They have an ebook and they've made a fortune from it."

I know many such business owners personally - people who have been making a lot of money for a long time from ebooks. I'm not talking about the business of ebooks, I'm talking about positioning you as the subject matter expert. I'm talking about positioning you as the go-to authority and generating so much free media as a result. For that to happen you need a real, physical book – one that can be purchased in bookstores and online. You can make an electronic copy of that available and sell it or give it away but the credibility comes from having created that from a physical book, which gained attention for you in the real world, not just the online one.

Think about it this way. Have you ever seen any daytime or late night talk show host interview anyone about their ebook? Of course not, it doesn't happen. When any news or talk shows bring on a guest, they establish that guest's authority instantly by saying "Our next guest is *so and so*, author of *such and such* book" and they hold a copy of the physical book up to the camera". You can't do that with an ebook!

The point to understand here is this. Regardless of what business you are in, even if it is all online – an influencer perhaps - you need a physical book to create your credibility and personal brand awareness and grab attention, to be seen as the expert, and then **use that to drive traffic to your online site.**

Now when it comes to sales, we all know you need to gain a prospect's attention and build trust. Nothing gains attention like a book. People are hungry for information, hungry for the answers they need. The internet has too much information and much of it contradictory and lot of it is from dubious sources. All that free information has produced many armchair experts that are of absolutely no value. So now more than ever, people want to deal with subject matter experts. The people or person who can show them how to find a specific solution to their problem or desire. So where do they get that from? Same place we always use to get trusted information from – a book!

Maybe you're old enough to remember that time before the internet? Before Google, Yahoo or Alta Vista. Where did people go then to get information? Books! Guess what, people still do so today. The advent of the internet has not killed the printed book like it has for many magazines and periodicals. If anything it has strengthened the demand and the need for them, especially during COVID lockdowns when the demand for books, especially *how to* type books went through the roof.

Since 2011 , the sales of physical books have increased year on year. Around 88% of all book sales are still physical books with only 12% being online, Kindle or Kobo type ebooks and audio books and many of those are versions of the printed book which came first.

Now here's the truly beautiful part: when someone reads your book, you then have their attention, completely and for at least a few hours – maybe not all at once but if they finish your book they have effectively had a one-on-one session with you for a few hours.

People pay far more attention to words in a book then they do to words online. Part of that is just our upbringing. We've been conditioned to believe that books are how to learn, from even before we began school, and that belief was only strengthened once we started school. We were taught that authors were the subject matter experts (or why else would they have been published?).

When someone is reading your book they are engaged with the written word. They do not suffer the same distractions experienced on the computer during a podcast or webinar or even a YouTube tutorial, where they have other tabs open and check their emails or Facebook, thereby only half paying attention to the message, and retaining little of it afterwards.

This means the information you supply in a book, your written words, will be far better absorbed and acted on, than <u>any other form of media marketing currently available.</u>

This lack of distraction means the reader is focused and becomes engrossed in your words, in your beliefs, in the way you posed the problems and then offered solutions to them. Believe it or not they hear your voice. If you write the way you speak, your personality comes through, your sense of humour, your thoughts and feelings, and that is what builds the incredible bond of trust. **After reading an author's words the reader feels like they know the author.**

What has effectively happened is you (the author) have just spent several hours with that person creating a bond. You built credibility and trust and positioned yourself as the authority, the go-to expert.

You've done it without ever having left your home or ever having spent one minute with that person. **It is the ultimate form of leveraging your time.** You publish and get just 1,000 books out there, then that's 1,000 people who can all be spending 2-3 hours at a time with you – *all at the same time* – all becoming advocates of you and your business. **That's the equivalent of spending 8 hours a day with prospects, every day of the year, for almost an entire year!**

By doing that, there is no need for 7 touch points. There is no need for a small sale to continue to build trust and hopefully work towards a bigger sale in the future – they already trust you. They already see you as the expert. You can straight away sell them into a much higher priced item. Because you are the expert, people expect AND accept that your prices are higher than your competitor and they pay them willingly.

Positioning yourself as THE Authority makes your competition effectively irrelevant.

So the book builds trust and credibility, positions you as the expert and it leverages your time. It also gets you access to clients you may not have otherwise been able to reach.

Now let's look at how to create your complete Authority Influencer Marketing book quickly and easily.

CHAPTER FOUR

How to create your Authority Marketing (even in under 3 hours)

> *Successful entrepreneurs don't wait for the perfect moment - they create it.*
>
> **Richard Branson**

CHAPTER FOUR

How to create your Authority Marketing (even in under 3 hours)

So when I revealed in the last chapter that the Number One Authority Marketing tool was a book, what happened? Did you find yourself thinking of any of the objections I listed in Chapter two? If so, did you deal with it as I suggested? Just remember to add "yet" to your limiting belief. So you say to yourself "I can't do that – _yet_".

In this chapter I am going to show you the quickest and easiest way to create this. **I will state how to complete the text for a book in just a few hours, even if you never touch a keyboard or pick up a pen!**

There are a lot of myths and misconceptions about writing a book, which is a good thing as the general public, more importantly your potential customers or clients, think that way and that's why they respect authors and perceive them to be so capable and credible. Let me dispel some of the myths here for you now so you can concentrate on creating your own Authority Influencer Marketing book.

The first two myths are the most important and most limiting for your subconscious but they are just myths. There is no reality to them, other than one you create for yourself. So please take the time to read and understand these two completely. When you do, you will see how easy it will be for you to do this.

Myth 1 – **I don't have anything to write about.** Or
I'm not the subject matter expert. Or
No one is interested in what I have to say.

This just simply isn't true. As you will read towards the end of this book, an eleven year old wrote a bestselling book. An 11 Year Old!!! If someone at eleven has enough life experience in a particular area to share in a book that sells well, then you most certainly do!

Your purpose for wanting to write a book should always be to share knowledge, to deliver great content. The easiest way to become wealthy is not to chase sales but to solve people's problems. When you can provide a solution or an easier way or alleviate some pain for others, money naturally flows to you.

Now regardless of whether you want to write a book for business or for a hobby or to share a life experience, the fact remains the same. If you have ever helped someone else, in business or in your hobby or through your life experience, then you are completely qualified to complete a book. If you have a passion about that thing and have spoken to others about it at length, then that is the crux of your book.

I will write more about that shortly. All I need you to think now is one simple thought –

By sharing what you know, could that help others?

If the answer is yes, then not only do you have a book people will read but a book that will be successful and will position you as an authority. It really is that simple as I will explain later.

After reading that explanation, most people are onboard and know, I mean truly know, that they have a book in them and now just want to know the best way to complete it. Some however state "But there are so many other people in my industry who all know the same thing, so how could I possibly be seen as the go-to authority?"

It is a great question and an understandable concern, that can be answered very easily.

In any business or in any hobby there are likely to be maybe 100 or more people as good as you at what you do, trying to compete for the same customers and clients that you want. That's true for every person in every industry. However, **there is only one you. No one else can tell YOUR story.** No one else can explain things exactly the way you intend to. Your way of explaining something is what will help you find YOUR audience.

This is a really important distinction you need to understand before going any further. So let me elaborate.

How many times have you seen the same information on a particular topic presented different ways? Which one resonated for you? Why do you think there are so many books on business that say the same things, just different ways? Same for weight loss books, fitness books, books on property or wealth creation or finance. We don't all learn the same way. We don't all understand the same things the same way. Many times it takes someone presenting the same information in a slightly different way for you to get it, or for it to 'click' as some would say.

What you need to do is tell YOUR story YOUR way and the people who 'get it' are the ones who are going to want more from you (much more about that in Chapter 10). For now all you need to know is the single greatest strength you have going for you, is that YOU are YOU! You are unique, even if what you are doing isn't!

Myth 2 – it takes a long time to write a book.

Well it does if you are Leo Tolstoy writing *War and Peace* with a quill pen back in the 1860's but this far into the 21st century there are a host of ways to complete a book quickly and with very little work – no need to write or type it if you don't want to.

We've had an author complete all the content for her book, including all the legal preamble at the front, everything at the back and everything in between, with cover design complete, proofread and typeset all in just 2 weeks. Anyone can do that if they follow the steps in this book and have the desire to complete it in that time.

Start with the end in mind. Who is your target audience? What sort of clients or customers are you trying to attract and which ones are you trying to repel? Keep a very clear idea about that as you progress.

Know what your Game Behind the Game is going to be (will be covered in chapter 6) as that will help direct you in the manner you want the manuscript to look.

Work out what each chapter heading should be and think about what points you would like to cover in that chapter, list them as bullet points. Then simply pick up your smart phone, tablet or computer and record yourself talking about each of those points. Do that with each chapter.

Be conversational. Don't think too hard about it and try and make it sound like an academic text. Just talk in your normal way as if you were explaining that concept to a friend. Don't edit yourself as you go. Just talk and let it flow. Other ideas may pop up as you go through this process, just let that happen. You can edit it easily later.

A *how to* book should be around 130 - 150 pages, definitely not more than 180. It is a statistical fact that if your book is more than 180 pages, less people buy it. If it's more than 150 pages, less people finish reading it and you really want them to finish your book as only then are they likely to recommend it to others or maybe even pass their copy to a friend.

Books of 130 to 150 pages works best. Some people think that's too short. However **the number of pages a book has does not determine its impact!** Look, people's attention spans are getting shorter. People want information and they want to learn quickly. So the best way to succeed is to just get to the point quickly. Just make sure you take enough time to establish your authority whilst doing so.

Remember that the reason for creating your book is to convince someone that you are the go-to authority, the person who can help them. To do that you should be as clear, concise, and as straightforward as possible.

So don't exceed 150 pages, which is about 30,000 words. Given the normal rate of speech, you should be able to speak that many words in 2 hours and 47 minutes. Then you just need to have that recording transcribed.

There are many ways to do that. I use *Otter.ai*, a fantastic real time transcription service that translates speech to text with reasonable accuracy. Some of our authors have used *rev.com*, a transcription service that at the time of writing cost US$1.50 per minute. So you could get a 30,000 word document transcribed for under $300.

You could instead have a person transcribe the audio file for you. You can find people to do that sort of work at *fivver.com*, *freelancer.com*, *upwork.com*, *guru.com* or any other platform where freelancers are looking for work. Be aware that many of them are probably using *Otter.ai* or *rev.com* anyway to do the job for them, so it's well worth investigating those options yourself before exploring having people to transcribe for you.

When you get the completed transcribed work back, read it. Doing so will help you identify any mistakes you may have made if you were distracted during the recording. Once you've made the corrections, I suggest giving it to a friend or colleague and have them read it to see if it makes sense. Our thoughts make sense to us because we understand the background or context. Sometimes when you speak your thoughts out loud, that context doesn't go with it. That can make some parts difficult for some people to understand. Identify those areas and clarify.

Ian Marsh created his book *The Inconvenient Truth About Business Success* in exactly this way. He merely recorded his thoughts re each chapter title and then had it transcribed. It took him less than half a day. The publisher did the rest. Ian knows how many clients that book brought him and the value of each of those clients and says that book (that he didn't even physically write or type) has generated close to $600,000 for his business.

 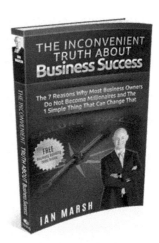

Ian Marsh and his book
The Inconvenient Truth About Business Success

The fact is there are a number of inexpensive options available to have an entire book written for you quickly and in your words. *In your words* is the important part here.

Myth 3 - is that you need to have a university education and degree to be taken seriously as an author and to be able to write in an academic way. Please don't do that. Have you ever read an academic paper? They are boring and full of jargon, suitable only for other academics in the same field. You want to write something that pretty much anyone can read and understand.

To do that, you want to write (or talk) as if you were conversing with a 15 year old. Talk the way you talk and let your sense of humour and personality come through. That is what the reader connects with. That's what builds that bond and trust between reader and author.

Keep in mind you are not trying to convey every single idea or piece of knowledge you have about the subject into one book. You are using the book to establish your authority and drive qualified clients or customers to your website. So throughout the book you should be directing them to that site for more information. Have items of interest on the website that they can get for free when they provide their name and email. This is the beginning of a quality customer list for you.

So not only do you NOT need a degree, you don't need to be well educated, great at spelling or good at written English at all to complete a book. Not in the day and age of spell checkers and you can even get programs to correct your grammar (Grammarly. com) but if you are having someone else transcribe it for you, then it doesn't matter what your English skills, penmanship, typing or spelling is like.

Dr John Gray, the author of *Men are from Mars and Women are from Venus*, is a self-confessed terrible speller and yet he sold over 40 million books! As he says "thank goodness for spell checker".

(Interestingly, the PhD John Gray has, came about by using the text for his book as his thesis to obtain his degree.)

The point to remember here is you are not trying to be the *best written* author, you want to be a *bestselling* author and the best positioned in your niche. You do that by following the steps in this book, not by completing a perfectly written academic script.

Myth 4 – You have to create the book yourself to have your name on it

Do you really believe Presidents and Prime Ministers have the time to sit and write (or even dictate) their memoirs? Have you seen some athletes who are struggling to put more than two coherent sentences together, come out with lengthy autobiographies leaving you wondering how did they ever manage that? Well the answer is simple. Those books have been ghost written.

Ghost writers are professional writers who interview you, learn your story and what the desired outcome is for your book. They learn about the way you speak, the type of language you use and the turn of phrase you spiel. From there they go and write a complete manuscript for you. The work is then published as your own, with your name on it - the ghost writers name does not appear anywhere on the book.

Some people view this as cheating or somehow unfair but if you have ever read a so called autobiography by enough world leaders, athletes or movie stars, I am certain at least one of those books was ghost written and you enjoyed it none the wiser. It still gave you the information you wanted and celebrity status for the person it was written about.

You can find ghost writers through an online search or through the freelance services listed previously. When choosing a ghost writer it is critical to check the quality of work they have done before. Prior to entering into an agreement with a ghost writer you should insist on seeing at least one book they have ghost written previously, as that will give you the best idea of how well the person writes.

Just be aware that of all the options listed here, ghost writing usually works out the most expensive. For the type of book you are considering, you could still be looking at $10,000 or more just for the basic manuscript. Of course you could probably have it done cheaper but the quality won't be the same and your professional image could suffer, defeating the whole purpose of having a book in the first place.

Myth 5 - To position you as the Authority, the book has to be about you

You don't need to be *the* expert to be seen as *an* expert. Remember - Authority and status is Passion, Perception and Positioning. If you've got the passion, you'll research and learn any shortages in the knowledge of a subject you want to publish a book about. Then you will know the subject matter for your book very well and be an expert on the content of your book, thus positioning you as the authority.

A great way to gain authority is to leverage off the credibility and knowledge of already established leaders and authorities in your field, which can be done through a compilation book. This is another easy way to have a book completed as you simply interview a select number of experts and have those interviews transcribed, compiled and published.

This then creates what is known as a Halo effect, meaning that if you are an author interviewing and writing about these successful and knowledgeable people, then by association you too must be successful and knowledgeable about that topic. At least that's how people perceive it and Authority is all about perception. Of course, the reality is you do become far more knowledgeable in that particular area because you just interviewed the experts and learnt from them by doing so.

A compilation book has so many benefits –
- You basically have others write it for you
- It leverages their credibility in building yours (Halo effect)

- Gives you an instant distribution network for your book
- Builds your back-end product, i.e. video and audio products and transcripts
- Builds your database
- Builds your profile as an expert in this area
- Connects you to the key people in the industry

See Chapter 6 for more information on how easily and successfully writing a compilation book provides everything listed above and can make you six figures profit and an international bestseller, <u>before</u> the book has even been printed!

Be aware that you can also achieve the Halo effect from whomever writes the foreword for your book. If a person of Authority writes the initial pages of your book – and that's the first thing people read, then as they read on they will always, subconsciously at least, associate you with that authority figure. Some of that person's credibility will instantly be transferred to you.

We have a technique we teach that allows our authors to reach famous people or celebrities who write the foreword to their book. Like Tracey Stranger who wrote *How to Overcome Stress Naturally* and had her foreword written by His Holiness the Dali Lama. What do you think that did for her credibility?

Tracey presenting her book to the
Dali Lama on his visit to Melbourne

Another person who used that same technique was Liz Dunoon whom at one of our workshops was asked "who would you like to have write a foreword for your book? If you could have anyone in the world write it, who would it be?"

Liz had children who were dyslexic. So she wrote a book *Helping Children With Dyslexia*, a simple title that tells you exactly what the book is about. She said, "I'd love Richard Branson to write the foreword."

It is important when selecting the person to write your foreword that they are aligned with your subject matter. Richard Branson suffers from dyslexia and has become hugely successful despite it so he was the ideal, inspirational choice to write the foreword for that book.

Liz was given one of the strategies we teach on how to get a foreword from someone like that and within six weeks, she had an absolutely stunning foreword, written personally by Richard Branson. What do you think that did for her business? It just skyrocketed because she had the credibility of a well known billionaire that is admired around the world for his Virgin brand and all the amazing things he has done as an entrepreneur, writing about his dealings with dyslexia.

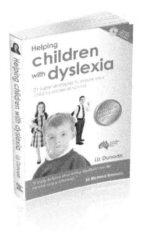

Some of that credibility transferred to Liz in the minds of those reading her book, even though she has never met Richard Branson. It was all done through just one of the strategies we teach and it has changed her whole life. She is now able to get her message and her products and services out to far more people, including her teaching programs which are all about helping parents, children and teachers, dealing with those suffering dyslexia. Due to her success, her programs are in use globally. Needless to say it has a massive impact on her business and on improving the lives of those affected by dyslexia.

Myth 6 – Authors only make money from the sale of the book.

This is probably the greatest belief around books and authors. I cover the different types of publishing in Chapter 11, but basically under traditional publishing authors only get a small percentage of the cover price of each book after it is sold. The publisher sets the retail price of that book.

Yes, some already highly successful authors can get a large advance paid to them prior to writing a book and then royalties on every book sold, after the initial sales cover the advance from the publisher. Do <u>not</u> expect that as a first time author.

Self published books allow you to keep all the profits from your book sales, however the number of books you can sell is limited as it is unlikely you will get self published books into book stores or on some other sales platforms.

Entrepreneurial publishing allows authors to make large amounts of money from the book before it is published and even more money once it is. It is what allows the most successful form of Authority Influencer Marketing and wealth creation to be distributed to the widest audience. Examples of how to make massive amounts of money before, during and after your book is published are covered in the next chapter.

Myth 7 – There is just no demand for printed books anymore

I find this the most entertaining of all the myths. I think this first started a couple of years after the Kindle e-reader first came out. The sales of that were phenomenal and so, many 'experts' made the declaration that paper was dead and ebooks were the way of the future and that all book stores and printers would go out of business as all print media went solely online. However, for books, quite the opposite happened.

Kindle e-reader reached its peak in popularity in 2011. Shortly after that sales dropped right off. This was in part because iPads and other tablet devices on the market had the functionality and practicality of an e-reader with all of the benefits of a laptop. Ebook sales continued as a result but they never, ever came anywhere near to replacing the printed book.

Why? Books are just too good, too abundant and too convenient to just be replaced in the same way the computer replaced the typewriter. People still enjoy going to bookstores. They enjoy picking up a physical book and looking it over. They enjoy the immediacy of it, the ability to see it now and know exactly what they are getting.

People like the fact that it is NOT a screen. When you work with computers all day and look at a tablet outside of that, when you want some down time, you don't want to be reading from an e-reader or tablet. A real book gives you a physical break from screens.

Since 2011 sales of physical books have increased year on year.

Really think about that one line you just read. For more than a decade physical book sales have increased every year, over the year before it. That peaked in 2021 with state enforced lockdowns in every state and most countries. However, even in 2022 after the pandemic shut-ins, physical book sales were still higher than any year pre COVID!

The reality is there are more books being produced and read now than at any other time in history - and there is no sign of that stopping. The largest distributor of books in this country recently moved to larger premises, offices and warehouse. They are far larger than they were 5 years ago and have room to grow by at least another 100%, as that is the growth they forecast this decade!

I have visited other commercial book printers we use and have seen the massive refurbishment in their facilities and equipment, which they have had to do to meet the ever increasing, global demand for physical printed books. The number of books being printed and distributed in this country on a daily basis is staggering, yet there is a strong demand for all of if it AND MUCH MORE TO COME!

The only thing that has changed is the way we obtain physical books. More people are ordering online and having the books delivered but they are still physical printed books. As I wrote in a previous chapter, around 88% of all books available here are still printed books. Ebooks and Audio books make up the smaller amount and many of them are simply downloadable versions of an already printed physical book!

So although physical brick and mortar bookstores may be finding it a little harder than it was 10 years ago, competing against the likes of Booktopia and Amazon and many others, they still exist because the printed book only continues to increase in popularity.

In Summary

Do not let these myths, these mistruths, ever hold you back from creating your own book. **Create your book the right way and dominate in your industry.** This has worked for so many authors and will for you as well, as long as you follow the straight forward tried and tested steps laid out in this book.

CHAPTER FIVE

Making money from Authority Influencer
Marketing before it is even finished

Real progress and success in Business does NOT come to those who work the hardest or the longest. It comes to those who find an easier way to accomplish things!

Start by finding the easiest thing that will generate the most impact in your business and do that first.

Andrew Carter

CHAPTER FIVE

Making money from Authority Influencer Marketing before it is even finished

An overview of the different methods of publishing needs to be covered to grasp the limitations of traditional and self publishing, and how through entrepreneurial publishing you have a great deal of scope to make massive amounts of money before the book is even printed.

For now, I just want to cover the basic techniques you can use, and the money that can be made through Entrepreneurial publishing. These basic strategies make tens of thousands of dollars for little effort. The more advanced technique will be covered in the next chapter, The Game Behind The Game.

Sell advertising in your book

The secret here is not to call it advertising in the book. Book distributors and the book stores they distribute to, are not fans of gross commercialisation of a book like that. They have a very traditional view of books which is, written words printed solely for the dissemination of information. However, when you are creating a book, there is only so much room in it and if you want to give your readers as much help as you can, then you owe it to them to provide other avenues to get more information and assistance. Therefore, you should include a resources section in the back of your book. You can sell pages in that section to other businesses to advertise their products or services.

What industry are you in? What are the relevant trade journals or magazines for that industry? If it doesn't have any, think about your ideal client. What magazines or papers do they read? Contact those businesses and ask for the advertising rates for their journal / magazine. You'll be surprised just how high some are - and remember that price is per issue so that ad is really only effective whilst that issue is new. That could be as little as one month and probably no longer than four months. In comparison a book has a shelf life of about 5 years.

When looking through those magazines have a look at who else is advertising there. Are any of those businesses complementary to your business without being direct competition? If so approach them, letting them know you are writing a book that is targeted at exactly the type of customer they want. State that you only have a select few positions to advertise complementary businesses in your book, businesses that would be of benefit to your readers. Tell them that they have a unique opportunity to advertise in your book and be seen by a large audience over a much longer length of time than in a magazine.

They will want to know what it costs. There are two ways to deal with that. If you have read the ad rate sheets for the industry periodicals and looked at what advertising that company is already doing with that particular paper or magazine, you already know roughly what they are currently paying for print advertising. Because the life of a book is about 5 years, you can substantially increase the price of what they are paying for magazine advertising. Depending on the industry, a page in a book for advertising can easily sell for anywhere from $10,000 - $15,000.

Sounds high? Be very aware that you can price too low and actually miss out on business. When it comes to advertising, people think spending more generates better results and so they are expecting to pay a certain price. If you come in too low it actually turns them off the deal. They think either your offering isn't good enough or you don't have enough faith in your product.

This is proven fact. I have seen this far too many times. We've had several authors tell us they tried this technique and didn't get one sale. When they tell us how cheap they are trying to sell it, we force them to raise their prices and try again – which they reluctantly do and are then pleasantly surprised how successfully it worked.

One of our authors used exactly this technique with her first book *How To Grow Your Business Faster Than Your Competitors* and generated over $40,000 by selling spots at $9,997 each. That's $40k net (after ALL expenses) she made before the book was even printed! She is just one of many of our authors who have succeeded using that method (even though she initially tried selling them at half that price and couldn't get any interest).

There is also another very effective way to sell advertising space.

Instead of selling it for the $10,000 to $15,000 as mentioned, you tell the client that you will provide a full page ad, with their logo featured prominently and all they have to do for that is pre purchase 500 books at half the retail price. This is a brilliant offer for several reasons.

First, they get the advertising at a relatively cheap rate and second, they receive something tangible from which they could actually make money. Think about it this way. If a regular *how to*, information type book sells for $29.95 and you offer the business wanting to advertise in your book, 500 books at $14.95, then they have paid you $7,475 for books which they can then sell direct to their clients or customers at full retail price and get their initial money back plus actually make a further $7,500 profit!

Now they may not choose to sell those books. They may instead give them away as a value add for some other product or service. They may even give it away as part of the beginning of their sales funnel as mentioned in the first chapter. They might hand them to prospective customers or clients at trade shows as a way of enhancing their brands credibility. Whatever they decide to do with them doesn't matter. You then have 500 books pre-sold.

Do that 10 times (10 different advertisers) and you have pre-sold 5,000 books which makes you a bestselling author in Australia. Being a genuine bestselling author is a big deal, yet alone achieving that before the book is even printed!

Note here I'm talking about genuine, bona fide, internationally recognised and respected bestseller here, <u>not</u> an Amazon bestseller. There is a massive difference. One requires thousands of copies of your book to have been sold. That is what builds your real credibility. Amazon have their own criteria for what they class as a bestseller and it changes continuously. It is used to generate more interest in some titles and to make more sales on their platform. It does not in any way refer to how good a book is or how well it sells in the real world and as such carries no kudos or gives you the credibility that being a true bestselling author does.

The argument can be made that for your positioning, to the uneducated public, having the Amazon bestseller title is better than not having a title at all. But real bestseller status is what you want to achieve and this book will show you how.

Bookstores will take on a genuine bestselling book over one that isn't as they know how much PR is generated for those and how that in turn creates extra demand for that book. Simply put, a bestselling book by definition is a great selling book. Book stores want great selling books. By creating one, you have generated your own best chance of success for your book and your business!

Even though there are plenty of sales platforms for your book, you need to get your books into bookstores as that is the easiest way to build credibility and generate massive FREE media and PR, which will be covered in another chapter.

Marketing your book is necessary regardless of whether you self publish or use a publisher. So why wait till the book is actually printed to start marketing it? You should start marketing as soon as possible.

Once you have your book title sorted, you can easily have a mock up book cover made with that title and some graphics (even if it isn't the same as what you finally decide on for the finished product). Use this to start promoting your soon to be released book. Advertise it on your website and start building pre orders. Offer a 20% - 50% discount for those who pre order before a certain date (creating a sense of urgency) or let them know the first print run is limited to a certain number of copies (creating a sense of scarcity) so they need to act now.

Approach other like minded businesses whose clients or customers could benefit from your book and offer it to them for a 50% commission, meaning all the ones they pre sell to their list of customers at full price, they keep half of it for themselves. This is a great incentive for them to advertise it to their list, a group of people you may not have otherwise been able to reach.

These pre sales bring in money before the book is printed and give you an idea of what demand there is for it, what sort of sales you can expect and what is working as far as promoting the book goes – you'll try different marketing techniques, those that are the most successful are the ones you will ramp up when the book is actually published.

There is a lot more money to be made from your book than what is listed here, *I mean a LOT more*. I cover that in the next chapter.

There is only so much more information than can be covered in this book. I cover a lot more in a unique live interactive workshop. To find out more go to - **www.MarketingInfluencer.com.au**

CHAPTER SIX

The Game Behind The Game – the greatest
use of Authority Influencer Marketing

> *Be seen as the Authority,
> not the sales person -
> Money follows and flows
> to Authority.*
>
> **Dan Kennedy**

CHAPTER SIX

The Game Behind The Game – the greatest use of Authority Influencer Marketing

Apart from gaining attention, building trust and developing your back end sales, undoubtably the single greatest reason you need a book is for something that we refer to as The Game Behind the Game. This is where the real money is to be made.

Most people believe that the sale of the book is how you make money but it isn't. A well written *how to* book of 150 pages can sell for up to $30. There are significant costs associated with designing and publishing a book which needs to be subtracted from the sales amount. If you go through a traditional publisher (learn more about the pros and cons of different types of publishing in Chapter 11) then you receive a very small percentage of the book price, around $1 - $1.50. Through self publishing you would make a lot more per book but it's unlikely you would be able to get it into bookstores.

So, depending on how you published, if you were to sell 1,000 copies, you've made somewhere between $1,000 and $25,000. Maybe that sounds like a lot but it's nothing compared to the amount of money you could have made and in fact should have made.

Successful authorpreneurs understand the real money comes from the attention, trust and credibility the book brings them and the other sales they make as a result of that.
This will be covered in more depth in the next chapter.

For now, let me show you how one book we published in the past made over $250,000 in just a few weeks with this strategy and how you could do exactly the same thing. In fact, we have shown many of our students how to do this and they have made anywhere from $50,000 to a couple of hundred thousand dollars doing it.

Darren Stephens, developed a book called *Top franchise SEO Secrets Revealed*. He was not a top franchisor himself and at the time was working with Dr John Gray on the *Mars Venus Coaching* franchise and wanted to get that established in Australia.

To give himself, and the new franchise *Mars Venus,* real credibility and build immediate trust, he used the compilation model I described in Myth 4 in Chapter 4, thus obtaining the Halo effect. If he and the brand were positioned amongst well known, trusted, established franchise brands and owners, he and his brand would receive similar credibility by association.

So he interviewed 14 franchisors, recorded the interviews and had those transcribed. Then he just laid out the transcripts in the book as a compilation of interviews. Effectively someone else (actually 14 someone elses) wrote the book for him because he just interviewed them and leveraged off the credibility of all these famous people that had well known franchise models. He gained the credibility alongside them as he was the author of the book.

It gave him an instant distribution network for the book, as he now had thousands of outlets (franchisee outlets) he could sell through. Having video recorded the interviews, he was able to build what are known as back end products – additional products that were created as a result of the book. He could compile and sell the video interviews or lift the sound from those for audio products and have them transcribed in different ways to make additional written products to the book.

Of course the book directed people to his website so that he could not only sell those additional products but importantly capture people's contact details, allowing him to build a database of potential people to sell other products to in the future.

So, just interviewing 14 people allowed that author to create a book as well as a whole stack of product, build a database, built him up as an expert in the franchising area and connected him with people in the industry that he normally wouldn't have been able to connect with. The book, the man and the franchise therefore became hugely successful.

In Chapter 5, I covered some ways entrepreneurial publishing will allow you to make a heap of money before the book is even published. Well, here's how it was done with the *Top franchise SEO Secrets Revealed.* **It actually generated over $251,000 in a couple of weeks, before the manuscript was even completed!**

There were 14 franchisors (actual people that own franchise systems) interviewed for the book. For those people to be included in this book, and hence give them far more exposure and credibility, they had to pre purchase copies of the book.

The concept is simple. As the author, he stated up front – "Look, I will do an interview with you, transcribe it and turn it into a great chapter for a book. We'll do all the artwork and place approved photos of you in it. We will do all that and feature you in this book alongside all these other people and generate more exposure and interest in your brand – and you'll most likely sell more franchises as a result.

All I ask is in order to get this book on the bestsellers list and get it (and thereby you) far more free publicity in the media, is that you pre purchase in advance 1,000 copies of the book. We'll give them to you at a cheap price, just over the cost of the book. The book will retail for $29.95 and you can buy copies for just $9.95 each. You can sell those books at the full retail rate (in which case you would actually make $20,000 profit) or you can give them away to clients as a promotional tool for your franchise or use them at trade shows and franchise conventions to build your credibility and maybe sell more franchises. Or you could give them to your current franchisees and let them sell them in store to make additional income."

So 14 contributors pre ordering 1,000 books each at $9.95 per book equalled $139,300

The author then approached other businesses that were relevant to the franchise sector and arranged to advertise them in the back of the book (this is not something you could ever do through a traditional publisher).

If you are looking at buying a franchise, you would need a franchise lawyer and maybe an accountant who understands that industry. You may need a franchising consultant, insurance agent and maybe even a specialist broker, one who knows the industry and can help find and structure an appropriate business loan.

So Darren found those people and offered them the chance to

advertise their brand, their goods and services in his book which had already pre sold 14,000 copies (to the franchisors). To be advertised in it, all they had to do was pre purchase 500 books at half price ($14.95). They could give those copies away as powerful, credible, third party advertising, or they could sell them at full retail price and make all their money back, plus that much again as profit!

15 advertisers agreed to this which generated another 7,500 book sales and $112,125

Subtract the cost of producing the books at the time and the money raised in just two weeks was **$143,925 profit**! The majority of small businesses in this country struggle to make that much profit in a year. This was done in just 2 weeks - and before the book was even compiled!

More importantly 21,500 books had been sold making this book an instant bestseller which makes it far more attractive to bookstores and generates massive free PR on the day it is released.

So those figures again were -

14 Contributors @ $9.95 a book x 1,000 books = $139,300
15 Advertisers @ $14.95 (50% off) a book x 500 books = $112,125
(The books retail for $29.95 each)
Total Revenue $251,425
Less costs of Production 21,500 books @$5 = $107,500
Total in Profits $143,925

So could you do that? Of course you could! How would you feel when you achieved that? Rich and proud of course. But that's just the beginning of the wealth a proper book written using our Authority Influencer Marketing strategy will create.

Although this particular book was on franchising, the same thing could easily be done on a collection of real estate agents. Same concept right, interview all the best real estate agents. Or maybe you're in the health and wellness industry and want to do something on that. You could go out and interview all the different health professionals - chiropractors, physios, massage therapists, naturopaths, nutritionists and so forth, and do a compilation book on that. The number of potential industries you could do this in is huge.

To prove the point that this one example wasn't just luck, that same author has done the exact same thing multiple times in different fields with similar results. Other graduates of our course have done the same. One of those was Pete Burden from New Zealand. The first book he did was *Media Training for Modern Leaders,* to build his authority and credibility as a media trainer. That book catapulted his business. The credibility it gave him generated so much extra clients and income.

For Pete's next book, he just copied the Franchise compilation model I just described but did it in his home country. Pete released *New Zealand's top franchise leaders Secrets Revealed*, doing exactly the same thing Darren did, and he generated over $120,000 in just two weeks, before the book was even printed! It has only increased from there.

Darren's Book   Pete's Book

So you can see it works each time you do it and you can cover many different topics and industries. You can do this on all sorts of things, it's really exciting what is possible.

Hopefully you're starting to understand the true power of a book and what it can do for you because it really can make a massive difference. Out of all the strategies as a marketer, all the things I've learnt and shared, all the things I've seen and with the businesses I've grown, **this is undoubtedly the number one strategy that works better than anything else.**

It doesn't matter whether you're an online business or offline business, this will make you stand out, gain massive credibility and grow your business exponentially with different strategies – the entire time **leaving you so far out ahead of your competition that they become irrelevant.**

The point of this chapter is to understand The Game Behind The Game and The Franchise book is a great example because in that instance The Game Behind The Game was multifaceted. What do you think it was?

Was it making a great 6 figure profit before the book had even been compiled?

Was it making the book a bestseller before it was printed?

Was it that by being a bestseller he could generate massive free media and PR?

Was it creating a huge database by tapping into the lists of other franchisors?

Was it the credibility he created for himself and his franchise through the Halo effect?

Was it the contacts /connections he made with the heads of Australia's largest franchises?

Of course it was all those things - but it was also much more. Those items listed above were the smallest part of The Game Behind The Game. The larger item was to get more exposure for the franchise he had introduced to the country and sell more of them. However, there was a Game Behind The Game of selling those franchises as well, which is where the real wealth actually lay.

Let me explain this one in detail because it breaks down exactly the real depth The Game Behind The Game can involve and the true magnitude of wealth it can create. Yet the concept is simple and easily achievable once you understand the power of it and start thinking that way. Remember, all of this starts with one simple thing – a book.

Dr John Gray. Mars Venus Brand

I'm sure everyone has heard of *Men Are From Mars and Women Are From Venus*. It and subsequent versions went on to sell over

40 million copies worldwide in over 150 countries, having been translated into 45 languages, generating over $1 billion.

John did become wealthy from the sales of his books but then far more so by developing a Game Behind The Game.

First and foremost, John used the contents of his book as his thesis to gain his PhD. Then turned some of the content from the books into seminars, workshops, video and audio products and speaking engagements. Matter of fact, John's speaking fees went from a couple of thousand dollars per speech to tens of thousands per talk. That is only possible because of the brand and the profile that comes from the book.

He went on to have a board game based on the brand, made and distributed by Mattel, which sold around the world generating another revenue stream.

The brand was franchised internationally, giving John another passive income stream from the franchising fees. This was the ultimate Game Behind The Game, selling licensing fees for the franchise in each country generated hundreds of thousands of dollars at a time. That in turn meant the company was later listed on the American Stock exchange for $61 million. All of these activities generated far more income for John than book sales alone ever did or could.

This all came about because one guy wrote a *how to* book on relationships and someone else was able to teach him about The Game Behind The Game.

It could only happen to John Gray you think? Not at all.

Konrad Bobilak attended our live workshop without having an established business. I mean he had no business at all – no premises, no business name, no leads, no idea, nothing. He learnt about the Game Behind The Game at the workshop and immediately understood it and was blown away by the potential of it. He decided right then and there to set up his ultimate lifestyle, to work when he wanted, where he wanted and pay himself $1 million a year (he'd never earnt anything like that before).

So during the workshop he started to craft his book around The Game Behind The Game. He completed the book, *Australian Property Finance Made Simple*, which became a bestseller. He created his websites and a YouTube channel around the book, designed to attract his ideal client and repel those who aren't, so he wasn't wasting his time dealing with the wrong people.

Using the book, he has created a company from nothing which is now paying him $1 million dollars a year income and yet to this day, his company has not spent even $1 on advertising. Not one!

As Konrad says, the real benefit of the book is that it reaches the type of clients he wants but could never get to. Airline pilots flying internationally read his book on the flight, then contact him upon landing wanting to do business. Expat surgeons looking to come back to Australia and trying to minimise their tax, read his book and then contact him ready to buy. These people are already avid fans and trust him enough to do multimillion dollar deals, even without meeting him face to face, all because of his book.

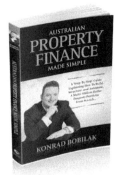 

Konrad's follow up book based on
the ongoing success of the first

To my way of thinking Konrad nailed it. **The real Game Behind the Game should be creating the lifestyle you want and living it.** However, everyone has a different idea about what they want their book to generate for them, so you should start thinking now what is the ultimate goal for you? Once you figure it out, you can craft your book to create that.

To find out many more ways to market and monetise your book, join me at a truly unique live workshop where I cover more strategies in far more depth and you leave with the complete blueprint for your Authority Marketing Book all mapped out.

Find out more at **www.MarketingInfluencer.com.au**

CHAPTER SEVEN

What are you selling next?

> *Approach Each Customer With The Idea of Helping Him or Her To Solve a Problem or Achieve a Goal, Not of Selling a Product or Service.*
>
> **Brian Tracy**

CHAPTER SEVEN

What are you selling next?

> *It is by solving people's problems that you ultimately become truly wealthy.*
>
> **Andrew Carter**

It doesn't matter if you are writing a book about your hobby, a personal life experience, or a business book, you need to be thinking – 'what will I sell next?'

You see you start with a book, either selling it or giving it away, but that's not where it ends as many authors think, rather that is just what gets the process started. The book establishes you as the authority and builds credibility. It builds your audience, people who like your message and trust you and *more importantly* **want more**

from you and are prepared to pay more to get it. Knowing how to fill that demand at each level is what produces your value ladder.

A value ladder is something that each business should have as a standard principle. From a marketing point of view, it is when you first capture someone's attention, what product or service do you have to offer them? Once they have purchased that, what do they buy next? After they have bought that, where do you take them, what's the next logical step? What's the next product or service that they should buy? Each one should be of higher value than the one before it. What is created is a staircase of services or products of increasing cost.

Each product or service you offer should offer a solution to a problem your client has or assist them in some way. Quite often, solving one problem for someone creates an additional problem and so you want to provide a solution to that as well. The best example I can give is when I show someone how to make far more money in their business, they now encounter additional tax issues that they hadn't encountered before. Some of them aren't able to keep up with the increased consumer demand because of poor systems and processes or lack of quality staff. Knowing what problems can come about from each problem you solve and figuring out how to deal with those, is the best way to create ongoing products or services for your value ladder.

Let's now look at a well established value ladder from someone you would know of - Tony Robbins. As you are aware, he is an amazing coach, author, speaker, influencer and he really has made a huge impact on the world with his message and his skill set in personal development.

That is what Tony is known for. He has built his entire brand around that. However the power of Authority and Influencer Marketing is such that when Tony wanted to change that perception in peoples mind, he was able to do so using the principles described in this book, and publish a book on an entirely new field of expertise.

Tony brought out a product around wealth creation because he wanted to be in financial markets, to teach people how to become wealthy using the stock market and other investments. For him to build a new value ladder he needed to create a book so that he gained the credibility for expertise and knowledge in the finance area.

It didn't matter that Tony was independently wealthy and had invested his money wisely to create even more wealth, he just wasn't known for that. Even though he had that knowledge, he wasn't perceived as the expert in wealth creation because his books had done such a great job of positioning him as the personal development expert.

To position himself in this new area he needed to publish a book about finance, to build massive credibility and trust, and he did that through association (the Halo effect).

Tony went and interviewed 50 of the top financial minds and created a book *Money – master the game*. He followed that up with a co-written book called *Unshakable – Your financial freedom playbook*. Having those books out there gave him the stepping stone to then be able to talk as an expert in the finance arena, as they positioned him as a real expert in that field.

Tony's value ladder starts with a book. From there, the next step is some of his digital programs, online courses or informative videos and workbooks. Then the next step up from those would be to see Tony at a live event.

Tony's live events range anywhere from $1,000 to $3,000 a ticket. So then, as the next logical step at those events, Tony will offer you to go to his *Date with Destiny*, his *Wealth Mastery* or his *Leadership Academy*. Different programs which are normally four or five day live in programs and they range anywhere from $10,000 to $15,000 each.

Continue ascending the steps to his highest level which is his *Platinum Partnership*. He normally has around 100 people in that each year and that's around US$85,000 to be a member. He is able to charge that much at that level because those involved are getting to be more up close and personal with him, with no distractions. It is a small group and they have a few trips away together each year and get direct access to him and his expertise for most of that time.

An example of Tony's value ladder

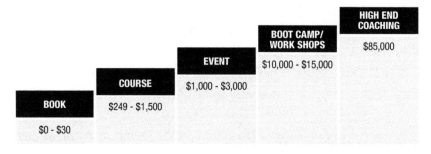

So do you have a value ladder in your business? If so, does it look similar to what I've shown here? If not, you're leaving a lot of income streams untapped and missing out on a lot of money.

If you don't have one, start one now. It's actually quite easy. The book is the first step. You might consider a membership site for $47 - $97 per month as the second step on your ladder. Video, audio or text used in creating the book can be developed into products for your third step on the ladder. Those packages might range from $297 to $1,997.

The next step can be a weekend workshop or boot camp teaching more by expanding on the information in the book. That could be around $1,997 - $9,997. Moving up from there you can set up your own one on one / group coaching services anywhere from $10,000 – $30,000 a year and then a mastermind or inner circle group which might range anywhere from $30,000 - $50,000 per person per year.

Some business owners struggle with the thought of charging that sort of money, thinking they are not good enough or somehow not worthy. However, If you have positioned yourself as the authority in the minds of your customers, some of them will be willing to pay that much money to get access to the expert, to get the answers they need and ultimately the success they want. $30k a year works out at $2,500 per month. Perhaps it's easier for you mentally if you think about charging it that way for a 12 month service.

Just keep this one simple thought in mind. *Those who can afford to pay a premium price will do so for a premium product, service or experience.*

Remember that you are not your ideal client or customer. Do not let your limiting beliefs around what you would be prepared to pay, stop you from offering it to others who would be glad to pay it, if it met their needs.

An ascension model or value ladder is something that you genuinely need to have in your business. Really think about it, think what is the next logical sale to step someone up to? Once somebody gets your product (your book), where do you take them next? What's the next step? Then what's the next step after that and then the next step? Because once a customer likes your product or service, they often want more and you have got to have more to give them, something that they can evolve up into, or they will go somewhere else.

Why? Well you built up the excitement and the anticipation and they want to take the next step, they want the next thing that will help them. If you don't have it they will look elsewhere to get it, meaning simply they could end up purchasing something from your competitor! Why would you do all the ground work just to let your competitors benefit from your efforts?

One of our authors (whose book is covered in a previous chapter) told me that although the need for additional products was made clear to her long before she finished her book, she never did anything about it because she didn't think it would apply to her (common misconception that most authors go through). Yet once the book came out, it didn't take long before readers started contacting her, congratulating her on the book and of course asking her what else did she have for them to purchase?

Now luckily for her, she ran a business with staff who could easily build websites and additional products quickly. If that hadn't been the case, she would have missed out on an incredible amount of money.

As she told me, "Let all authors know that once their book is sent to the printers, they need to start working on their value ladder and creating other products or services to sell because the demand will come – and you want to be standing with your surfboard ready when that tsunami hits, so you can catch that wave, rather than be wiped out by it!"

Once you've established yourself as the brand, as the authority, there is no end to back end products and services you can offer under that brand through many various arrangements. You'll find more to help you with that in Chapter 10, the five P's.

If you'd like far greater exposure to understanding how to create a book, a value ladder and The Game Behind The Game, please go to **www.MarketingInfluencer.com.au**

CHAPTER EIGHT

How to use Artificial Intelligence to build your Authority

We are all ignorant to some degree – until someone shows us a better way to do things. The successful try the better way - the rest choose to remain ignorant.

Andrew Carter

CHAPTER EIGHT

How to use Artificial Intelligence to build your Authority

No book like this could ever be complete without discussing Artificial Intelligence (AI). It is being hailed as the answer to everything but it simply isn't. It is without doubt the single greatest advancement online since the beginning of the internet and its future is going to be something phenomenal but for now we have to concentrate on what it really is, compared to what it is perceived to be, and how to make it work for you.

The argument is that all books, all screen plays, answers to university exams, everything, can be written by AI. To a certain, very limited extent, that is true but we need to look at this in more detail, for disregarding the strategy outlined in this book and relying purely on AI to write your book, simply will not create the authority you are trying to establish. In fact, it will actually damage it.

AI's greatest strength is the ability to access large volumes of text and present it in a way requested by the user. The more sophisticated the result you are after, the more steps or layers are needed to obtain the closest result.

So if you know how to use something like ChatGPT / ChatAI correctly (most people don't) you can get it to complete a university exam on law or medicine. This is where it is best, regurgitating large volumes of well known text. However, writing a book, especially one that will establish your authority, is slightly different.

There is a plugin for ChatGPT to write a book. Feel free to use it, I'm sure you will be completely underwhelmed by the result. There are a number of factors you need to consider.

No AI program knows you. It does not know your background, your experiences, how you felt at certain times. Ask ChatGPT to write about you or just about a moment in your life, it can't do it. The reality is that it will never be able to do it – how could it?

It is precisely YOUR experience and how YOU felt and reacted to certain events in YOUR life that have made YOU the person you are today. It is those experiences and the way you dealt with issues in your past and how you describe them, that people will connect with. It is in fact what will make you the go-to authority in the minds of those that read YOUR words – so make sure they are YOUR words.

Current AI has some severe limitations around what we are trying to achieve here. Of course the technology is going to continue to improve and plugins will continue to make it easier with you not having to create as many (or maybe any) layers to generate what you need – but remember, for you to be seen as the Authority, the influencer, the Go-To person, the reader needs to hear YOUR voice when they read YOUR words. Your style, your humour your personality all come through from you speaking your book and having it transcribed as opposed to having ChatGPT create a generic type book.

Here is a classic example that was done by a social marketing expert friend of mine who was trying to make the same point I am here. She writes -

…not surprisingly (given it was developed in Silicon Valley), ChatGPT writes "in American". It's pretty much clueless when it comes to writing something that will appeal to an Australian audience. If you don't believe us - check this out… We asked ChatGPT to write something a typical Australian would say.
Here's what we got:

"The other day, I was chockers and in a bit of a flap, so I decided to duck into the bottle-o for a coldie to help me chillax. As I was wandering up and down the aisles trying to decide between a schooner or a slab, I saw a fellow aussie mate who gave me a friendly g'day. We got to yarnin' and he said he was heading off to a barbie with his relos, but he wasn't sure whether to bring his sunnies and his togs, or his jumper and his brolly. I told him to pack everything but the kitchen sink, you never know what kind of weather you're going to get these days. He laughed and said fair dinkum, and we both went on our merry ways."

I mean seriously! How many Australians do you know who speak like that?! It's a caricature, or maybe a comedy act - it's certainly NOT how you want your Facebook ads or any representation of you, to sound!

The moral of the story? DON'T get ChatGPT to write your Facebook ads (or Authority Book), unless you want them either overhyped or cringe-worthy.

The good news though, is that there are LOTS of ways you CAN use ChatGPT for your marketing. Designing content, coming up with topic ideas for Lives and Reels, finding your audiences, AI works incredibly well if you know the RIGHT way to use it. It will save you loads of time (and boost your profits) if you do it right…just don't end up being "chockers and in a bit of a flap"!

So AI definitely has a place in all this, just not the way you initially thought and definitely not to write the book that is going to position you as the Go-To Authority.

In chapter 4, I mentioned the best way to complete the manuscript for your book was simply to talk about your experience and have it transcribed through the likes of Otter.ai – which is actually an AI program. I actively encourage you to use that type of AI for the fastest creation of YOUR story.

As fare as having AI completely write your book for you, accept now that all the hype and all the new programs hitting the market, are not the answer for producing your Authority Influencer Marketing book. If you are having your spoken word transcribed by a program, then you are using AI. This is the most important part of establishing your status, so do it properly. Do it the way outlined in this book.

You should be using other AI tools to help create content, get ideas, produce documents or checklists or any number of back end products you can use or sell or combine as give aways for your sales funnel or package to value add with your book. I will cover content creation for those in the next chapter and list some AI tools you can use for that at the back of this book but I won't go into great detail as there is plenty of information out there about AI, you just need to know the limitations and learn how to make it work best for you, in the areas that will make the most difference for your business.

I have seen many small ebooks written purely by ChatGPT and generally speaking aren't too bad. They are however very generic, which is to be expected as that is the very nature of AI.

If 100 people all type into ChatGPT they want a 30 page ebook on the best tips for marketing a business, what do you think would happen? The best tips as determined by AI remain the same and so we will get 100 books all of a very similar layout, spruiking the same points, much the same way.

Yes, AI's big claim is that none of the books would be identical and there would not be any copyright infringement in them (legally this is a very grey area that will eventually be contested in some landmark law case) but that's not the point. You need to stand out. You need to be seen as an individual. You need to be seen as the Authority. To just simply produce generic material means readers see you as just another one of the many. So don't do that. Be yourself and stand out!

If you are really stuck for content ideas for your book, then type that into ChatGPT. If it comes up with some ideas you like but want help writing about, copy one of those ideas and then paste it back into ChatGPT with a request to expand on that idea. Now the AI is creating some meaningful text for you. It is important to read what it produces and then personalise it. Add your thoughts, feeling or experiences around this into the text itself. That's what makes it yours. That's what makes the book and you stand out and that's what the reader identifies with.

Know that when using ChatAI, you can't just type in something basic or generic and hope for a great result. That's not how to get something useful. You must include specific prompts done the correct way. Here's what the company says about that -

Writing a prompt is one of the most important steps in your AI process. In order for ChatAI to do its job correctly, it needs good instructions. The better the instructions, the better the response ChatAI gives you. Let's start with the basics.

A prompt is a set of instructions or discussion topics you give to the AI to respond to. A prompt can be a question, statement, or command intended to spark a creative and engaging response or conversation.

A prompt has two key components: the context and the task.

The context is the background for the task. This can include the perspective, personality, or audience that informs ChatAI how to do something. The context can also be text you provide the AI to use or reference for the task.

Examples:

You are a personal trainer and former world cup winner.
- Design a training plan for an attacking midfielder to train for 5 days a week. Make 30 unique plans that are fun and engaging. Include both soccer skills and fitness training.

You're an 11th-grade history teacher.
- Create a 10-question quiz that tests a student's understanding of 18th-century European geography.

Always use proper grammar and spelling in your prompt.

The task is the action you want the AI to take. This includes things like summarising or analysing text, designing a plan, writing a story, solving a math problem, or asking a question related to the text you provide, etc.

Remember, the less detail you provide, the more assumptions the AI model needs to make. By providing a clear context and task, ChatAI can help you breeze through tasks in no time.

The information provided in this chapter is more for creating written products or courses as back end products to your book.

For more information on how to use those products, see the next chapter and the AI resources at the back of the book.

CHAPTER NINE

How to use your Authority Marketing
to maximum effect

> *The ability to influence
> people without irritating
> them is the most profitable
> skill you can learn.*
>
> **Napoleon Hill**

CHAPTER NINE

How to use your Authority Marketing to maximum effect

There is so much more to having a book than most people ever realise. Most people think that a book is just written information easily disseminated. That is just the very tip of the iceberg, they don't see the massive impact that it has underneath.

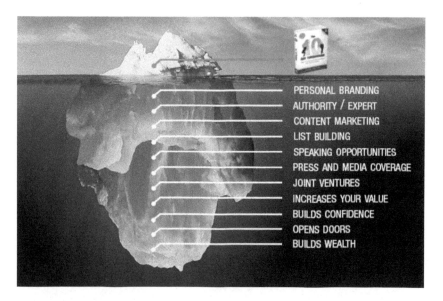

PERSONAL BRANDING
AUTHORITY / EXPERT
CONTENT MARKETING
LIST BUILDING
SPEAKING OPPORTUNITIES
PRESS AND MEDIA COVERAGE
JOINT VENTURES
INCREASES YOUR VALUE
BUILDS CONFIDENCE
OPENS DOORS
BUILDS WEALTH

The book helps build your personal brand. It positions you as the authority, the expert. We all know that experts and authority figures get paid more money. It gives you massive credibility as it is not you going around claiming to be the expert, that is just how people perceive you by default after your book is published.

Your book helps you, content marketing wise. If you have a book, you can pull content from it and use that for social media posts, marketing, advertising and for articles in magazines. You can expand on chapters in the book for content on your membership site and so much more.

It allows you to build a list of high quality prospective clients, people far more likely to step up your value ladder with any current or future offerings. Without a list, you don't have a business.

It gives you speaking opportunities. I know many people have a fear of public speaking and you might be one of them. I'm not saying you have to act on every opportunity publishing your book gives you but if offered speaking gigs, it is something you should consider. As a published author you can command good money for just a single talk of one or two hours. Even better if you use that opportunity to promote your book to get more people going to your website, growing your list and stepping up your value ladder.

Speaking is something you have been doing all your life, so why be afraid of it just because it's now going to be in front of a group of people? You have the opportunity to prepare and practice what you will say. You already know the topic well, as that is what you wrote your book about. An opportunity to get paid well to talk about something you are passionate about is not an opportunity that should be dismissed lightly.

I've mentioned before that you can attract a lot of free media and PR after you initially market your book. Again, it is just one of those surprising things that happens when you are published. Even though you have the same knowledge you did before your book was available, the media are only interested in hearing from you once you are a published author. That's when they perceive you as the expert.

The book allows you to do joint ventures with people because those people see you as the expert, as the authority, and they want to partner with you because they see that as adding value to their business or offering. So the book increases the value of your brand, your business and your value overall.

The book leverages you better than anything else out there. It is gaining the attention for you, building the rapport and trust for you, it can even be doing the selling for you – all without you ever leaving the house, making cold calls or having to visit clients, or send reps to do the same!

The book builds confidence. Not just other people's confidence in you and your brand, it actually builds your self confidence as well. This is probably the least known of all of the benefits of publishing a book, so I'll cover it in more depth here.

We've helped hundreds of authors through a proven system of writing and publishing an Authority Influencer Marketing book and there is no doubt that it also serves as a self development course. Nearly everyone has some initial doubts about writing a book, they wonder if they are worthy, or if they are knowledgeable enough. Most wonder "what if I fail?" or the other side of that, others have concerns about being successful, as that can create a fear of the unknown for some.

Having a system to follow basically guarantees success, so failure is never really an issue. That said, the would-be author still works through each of those doubts but as they pass each milestone through the system, doubt ebbs away and confidence grows. They can see this working. They can see the end in sight. They know they are going to do this.

Then one day they finish their book. This is a major accomplishment and the excitement and the sense of achievement justifiably results in a feeling of immense pride. That feeling multiplies exponentially when they actually hold their published book in their hands for the first time. I'm sure you've considered how incredible it will feel to hold your completed book for the first time.

So just having finished the book sees your self esteem and confidence increase. Then, because of the confidence that people have in you as an author, your confidence rises more and you attract more into your life, you attract more wealth and success, which makes you even more confident. Thus creating a self sustaining cycle that opens up doors that you may never have dreamt of or ever thought were possible.

So does all that happen just by writing a book? No. It has to be published, it has to be promoted and distributed and you have to know how to use it.

There are some powerful ways to use your book to build impressive back end sales as well as true long term wealth through The Game Behind The Game that I covered in Chapter 6. However, to begin with, all coaches, influencers, entrepreneurs, indeed every business owner, should **use a book as a business card,** if they really want to stand out from their competitors.

Think about it like this. If you are at a conference with 50 other people in the same industry as you, but you have written a book, and someone seeking those services enters the conference room and approaches all 50 of you, they will walk away with 49 business cards from all the others and a book on the subject from you. When they get home, do you think they are going to bother with 49 business cards, looking up the websites to see who suits them best? No, of course not. All 49 cards end up in the bin and the prospect thumbs through pages of your book – or reads it in its entirety, then contacts you already presold. Especially if you take a minute or two to personally sign the book at the time - that leaves an indelible impression.

If you are meeting someone for the first time, even if just in passing, whether famous or not, and they are someone you would like to build a relationship with, then give them a free copy of your book and sign it and write your phone number under the signature. In most cases you'll hear back from that person the following day.

This of course means you should be travelling with copies of your books at all times. You never know who you are going to meet or what opportunities will come from giving someone your book. Make sure you have a handbag, man bag, briefcase, backpack, whatever, big enough to comfortably carry some books with you.

Once you find a way to reach your ideal client (through your website or customer list or a Joint Venture deal with others, or through some form of targeted advertising online or offline) offer to send them the book at no cost, as long as they pay for postage and handling. Your ideal client gets a book at far below retail cost, however they are more likely to read it as they have had to pay something for it (postage).

This is worthwhile to you if you have built a great back end in the book (additional products for sale), as the money you can generate is tens of thousands of dollars - or in the case of Konrad Bobilak and his real estate book, millions of dollars. For that reason Konrad would be happy to never make a dollar on the sale of his books – he doesn't need to. He just needs to get his books into the hands of the right people. This 'free book' strategy has been used very successfully by some of the biggest names out there, so you should consider doing the same.

Having a book is the ultimate closer in any meeting or negotiation. When you get to the final close and you are dealing with objections, no matter what they come up with, you can simply counter it with "yeah, but I wrote the book on the subject". Do you know how powerful and complete a finish that is?

We've had authors do exactly that. In one case closing a very lucrative contract that was about to be awarded to a competitor. Greg Cassar was told he and the other final tender they had selected were close to each other in price (multi six figure contract) but the company was leaning towards the other tender. When asked why should they do business with him instead, Greg simply stated "I can't speak about the other company. All I can tell you is I wrote the book on this". He handed them a copy of his book *Our Internet Secrets* (a compilation book with him on the front cover) and they awarded him the contract.

Greg Cassar on the front cover of Our Internet Secrets

Do not underestimate the power that being a published author gives you in regards to being seen as special, as the go-to person, authority or expert in that field – and what that can do for you and your business.

Your book will make you an Influencer with celebrity status so that you can get media attention, in all forms of print, on TV, radio, podcast interviews and traction on social media platforms and **Make You More Money** - but first you have to get it out there.

Promoting your brand

Jason Smith founded Back in Motion, a physiotherapy business, with more than 60 locations around the country and over 350 staff making them the largest such group in Australia. The business turned over around $60 million a year.

Jason understood the Game Behind The Game and how to use the book to promote himself, his franchise and his franchisees.

He actually had 13,000 copies of his book printed in the first print run, and literally received over half a million dollars worth of free media and PR. As you can imagine, that absolutely transformed the company.

I'll explain this in detail as this is the ultimate way to use a book and I'm sure you will get some great ideas as to how you could implement some of this yourself.

The initial book *Back In Motion* came out with Jason Smith on the cover as he was the author and the franchisor. This was the version that went into book stores. There was enough room left on the cover to provide other opportunities. First, was to list the primary advertiser on the cover and earn far more from them. You might be able to get an endorsement from the authoritative body in your industry and place that on the front of your book which would give the book extra credibility, basically a Halo effect.

Original Cover   Original Cover
with advertiser

In order to promote each of the franchisees, the original book cover was adapted so that different franchisees had their picture on the cover alongside Jason, with their name under Jason's, appearing as a co-author for that book. Each of those franchisees received copies of those books for their own local marketing in their area and that gave them their own credibility and prestige in their local markets. You might be able to do something like that as well.

That took the brand to a whole new level and generated media on a scale Jason initially could not believe. When asked about it, Jason said –

"We've had more than 90 discrete pieces of media exposure directly as a result of the book, as a device, to try and get us into a conversation with the average consumer. It's probably hard to judge the commercial value of the media exposure we've gained, but I think conservatively what's happened is we have been given opportunities that you simply could not have bought.

Therefore, it's really immeasurable value and the sort of advertising dollars that it would have cost to just get into some of the publications and some of this media exposure, if we could buy it, probably would be many hundreds of thousands of dollars worth, so for us it is a no brainer. It was absolutely a triumph in terms of the commercial strategy and it's something that we still think has many years of tentacles in terms of other opportunities we can launch off the back of it."

Jason's Game Behind the Game was to increase the total number of franchises, then sell the company as his exit strategy. The book allowed him to gain more franchisees and help them build successful businesses, increasing the value of the brand overall. Which in turn allowed him to sell to an ASX listed health group for $125 million!

That's why I make such a big deal about The Game Behind The Game for authors, because that's what can be achieved – and yet it all starts with a book, one single book.

Generating Massive FREE PR

That example from Jason Smith of Back In Motion generating free media and PR is typical of many of our authors. You need to initially promote your book either yourself with press releases and sending them to media outlets, tying your book to a topical subject at the time, or have a professional PR company do it. Then once the press around your book takes off, it just seems to feed itself and you find yourself getting far more coverage with less effort. Since most media is syndicated, get it into one form and the other forms pick up that same content and run with it. That is far easier for them than having to generate new content all the time.

I'm going to show you some examples of others who used the book to generate massive FREE PR. It is mind blowing just what is possible and how much exposure you can get free and what that can do for your business. The end result of that is of course that you then have a whole host of people coming to you wanting to pay for your product or service, that are completely pre sold on you. Not only do you have the authority that comes from being an author but now the added credibility of being an author that the media has covered.

Merryn Snare is another one of our bestselling authors. She is a psychologist and stress management expert who wrote a book called *Annihilate Stress and Anxiety*. One of the things that she really wanted to do was meet Oprah, so she wrote about Oprah in her book. Well, the amazing thing was because of the book, guess what? She actually got to meet Oprah! That came about because she had her book featured at the Academy Awards. It was selected to be included in the 'goodies bag' of samples that are given to all the A-list celebrities who attend the Oscars. So Merryn's book ended up in the hands of famous celebrities like Liam Neeson, Meryl Streep, Reese Witherspoon, Oprah, Bradley Cooper plus many more.

When Oprah came to Australia, Merryn was able to attend one of her events and was able to connect with Oprah as the author of a book Oprah had received through the goodie bag, allowing her to meet Oprah and have her dream come true.

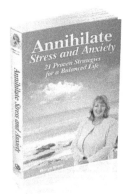

"How To Write A Bestseller Author"
Merryn Snare & Oprah Winfrey

Merryn received a huge amount of media exposure from being an Australian author, who had her book included in a goodies bag at the Oscars that ultimately end up in the hands of the biggest names in Hollywood. That amazing exposure helped boost her brand and her credibility in a way she never imagined possible. You literally can't buy press like that, meaning it is effectively priceless.

We've had other authors also have their books featured in the same show bag in different years, generating increased media exposure for them and their brand as well.

Karina Francois was a naturopath wanting to know how she could grow her clinic, an actual physical bricks and mortar business. Well to grow any business, you need to be seen as the authority and that comes from being the author of a book. She wrote on the topic that she's passionate about, health naturally.

Her book was *Clean Food Clear Thinking - how to change your body, change your mind*. She ended up becoming one of our bestselling authors and really expanded her business in a massive way, because she received so much free media. Here are just some of the examples.

She was initially written about in Good Health magazine and then other physical magazines and lot of online magazines. So she received lots of publicity, literally hundreds of thousands of dollars worth, completely free. From that, Karina then became a regular columnist in women's magazines, giving her even far more credibility and brand exposure.

She branched out with her own herbal tea range and that sell all around the world (see the following chapter for how to use white label products in your business). That book had such a major impact and allowed her to do so much more as THE authority figure, because now she's not just a naturopath, she's actually a bestselling author - the go-to expert or Authority, which carries far more weight.

Jo Munro, another one of our authors, came to one of our courses and was asked, "what is your passion?" She said "Shopping", so it was suggested, she do a book about her shopping tips, basically a shopaholics guide. She wrote a book titled *Savvy Shopaholic*. Jo never even imagined what impact that was going to have on her life.

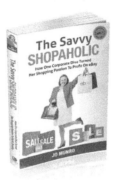

When the book came out, all of a sudden TV stations rang up asking, "can we get you for an interview to tell us what your hot shopping tips would be?" She appeared on daytime TV doing exactly that. It was a huge success, so they started using her as a regular on certain TV spots. They had her come on and do shopping tips, how to get the best prices, what retail stores had bargains on at the time and all these different things. She has done literally hundreds of TV appearances.

She was then approached by a jewellery manufacturing company who had seen her on TV and recognised her brand as the shopping ambassador, the expert, based on her authority from writing a book. They offered her a paid opportunity to become the brand ambassador for a jewellery line they labelled the *Jo Munro collection*. They created a whole line of beautiful jewellery to be sold online under her own personal brand. How would you like your own personalised jewellery line, just from having a book published?

A book can open so many opportunities that you never saw coming or that you never thought possible. Jo certainly didn't see a jewellery line named after her. All she had to do was put her face on it and be the brand ambassador for that jewellery collection. So again, these are the things that can come from being an author.

Suzanne McTier-Browne, another one of our authors, literally had an entire page written about her in the paper before her book was even printed. She had just been talking to the person seated beside her on a flight home. She mentioned she was in the middle of writing a book and it just so happened the guy she was talking to was an editor of a newspaper and decided to run the story, because her book *Drug Free Pain Relief* was a great story. The entire story was run before the book even came out, which gave her heaps of free publicity and created a demand for the books as soon as they were available.

From the celebrity and credibility she gained from being the author of that book, she then had the privilege of meeting and interviewing Mel Gibson, the actor and other celebrities. She was from a small town in Queensland, Australia and is now recognised for her work internationally.

Suzanne on stage with Mel Gibson

Build a massive list of buyers

The next thing that I want to cover is how you can generate a list of hot buyers. One of the things that you want is to have people that are coming to you that are already hot, that are already wanting to buy from you, so you don't have to try and educate them or convince them that you've got a great product or service or can be trusted, they're already coming to you with that in mind.

The book is just a tool, an incredibly powerful tool but keep that in mind and use it as such. Your book should be driving people to your website at every opportunity. If you self publish or use the Entrepreneurial publisher, you will be able to promote your website on the back of the book and at the bottom of every page if you wanted to (traditional publishers will not let you do that). This at least makes readers aware of your site where they can go to for more information.

I suggest you deliberately drive readers to your site. At the end of each chapter you can inform the reader that there is more information available at the website. Or you can have more graphical information on the site. Rather than clog up the pages of your book with graphs, charts and diagrams etc (especially in black and white) those would be much better shown on your website in a larger, easier to read format and in colour.

What about if you're trying to explain a concept or a 'how to' in your book? Reading can sometimes be a hard way to comprehend a difficult, abstract or esoteric concept. Why not direct the reader to your website to see a video demonstrating exactly what you mean? A picture may tell a thousand words but a video explains everything.

For people to get access to the page on your website with all this extra info, they have to enter their name and email. If you want to make sure they actually have your book as well, you might also get them to enter the first word on page 17 or some such. If they don't enter that info, they don't get access to all the extra freebies. This is how you build a list of hot leads, people who have read your book and are genuinely interested in you and what else you have to offer.

You also want to capture the details of people who haven't yet bought your book. You might drive people to your books online ordering page through other forms of online or offline advertising. On that order page have something of real value to give away, a free download, maybe the best chapter from your book.

Konrad Bobilak does this with staggering success. He gives away the three best chapters of his *Property Finance made Simple* book for free. People have to input their details to download them, so he is building his list but he is also increasing his chances of having someone purchase his book. The chapters are well written and incredibly informative so people reading them think "if the stuff he is giving away is this good, how great must be the stuff you pay for?!"

Another powerful strategy is to give away the first month of your membership course. You get their name, email and credit card details – and if they don't cancel after the first month, you have their monthly payments for the length of the course or until they unsubscribe.

The point is to think creatively. Create great content you can give away if people sign up. If you use the right software, you can actually have your list segmented. Those who enquire about your book go on one list and you can send them regular updates and useful information until they do buy, at which stage they then get transferred over to another list.

At each stage as they move up your value ladder you move them to a list that caters to the next thing you want to sell to them. At each stage **under promise and over deliver**. Don't give away substandard free PDF ebook reports that you received free from somewhere else (or are completely generic books developed by tying the same old keywords into an AI generator). That only damages your credibility and brand and ultimately deteriorates your authority status. Authority and professionalism go hand in hand.

At each stage you have to ensure you are giving great products or service to your customers, better than your competitors. You need to ensure that the next thing you are selling to them meets their needs and exceeds their expectations. This is how you remain number one in your customers minds and have them continually coming back for more.

To see an example of what I have just written about and to find out how you can learn far more than what is written here go to **www.MarketingInfluencer.com.au**

CHAPTER TEN

The Five P's to success

> *Whether you flounder or flourish is always in your hands — you are the single biggest influence in your life. Your journey begins with a choice to get up, step out, and live fully.*
>
> **Oprah Winfrey**

CHAPTER TEN

The Five P's to success

By now you should have a very clear picture of how you are going to achieve authority status and increase wealth, as you now have most of the pieces of the puzzle. To recap and bring it back to its simplest components, let's lay out the pieces of the puzzle here and get clear on the steps needed to go from where you are now, to where you want to be.

It comes down to the five P's

Passion – you already have that and proven it by reading this far. You are already passionate about the field or business that you are in. It may be that you are completely passionate about a hobby or a cause or a life changing experience. We've had plenty of authors passionate about those things, who used this same model and generated money from it. You can see a list of the non-business types of books we have covered in the following chapter. So regardless of what it is that you are passionate about, all that matters is that you are passionate.

Positioning – what your book will do for you. It takes your passion and positions you as the go-to authority or expert in the area you are passionate about. Let's look at the concerns most people have around this:

I am not the expert – no, maybe not *the* expert but you can be *an* expert and still be seen as the go-to person in your field. You already have certain knowledge, you know what your book is to be about, so any knowledge you are lacking will be made up through research. Once you've done that, you are an expert, at least as far as the content of your book goes.

That doesn't apply if I've had the book ghost written – yes it does. The ghost writer will do the research and you are going to read the manuscript before it is published, then you will have that knowledge. (Please don't be like a certain Olympic athlete who may or may not have opened the Sydney 2000 Olympic games, who clearly had her biography ghost written but then didn't bother to read it. She got plenty of free PR as a result of her book being published but when asked questions from it, simply wasn't able to answer them – that's not a credibility builder, that's a credibility buster!)

I don't feel comfortable telling people I'm an expert – that's fine, most people feel that way and even if you did feel comfortable doing it, I would advise you against doing so. In this country at least, it is seen as bragging and works as a detractor meaning people are actually less likely to trust you. The real brilliance of a book is IT promotes you as the expert. IT positions you as the authority, as the leader in your field, without you ever having to say those words yourself. Some people who will have read your work will be so impressed and actually tell you that you are an expert. You may politely disagree and then those same people will see you as humble and even more trustworthy.

A book truly is the number one Authority and Influencing Marketing tool you can have.

<u>Promotion</u> – this is quite involved and comes from a number of sources.

As already covered, Free PR can become self perpetuating. You do need to market your book heavily initially and do standard press releases to the media – who are always keen for new content, more so when it comes from an authority – an author. They love to talk about a topic that a book has just been written on and say "we have the author of that book joining us now".

That first bit of media will feed into other media as much of it is syndicated anyway or lazy journalists just look at what their peers are doing and copy it. In the future, whenever anything related to that topic comes up, the media tend to come back to you, for at least a quote, as you are seen to be the expert, and each time they state you are the author of your book on the topic.

What about having others promote for you? Not just your book but your products. Joint Venture partners can promote you, your book, your brand and your products to their lists in exchange for a percentage of the sale. It's basically giving away part of a profit from a sale you would never have made if it hadn't been for them. Many truly successful entrepreneurs who really understand their back end and what the lifetime value of a client or customer is worth to them are comfortable giving away 100% of the initial sale, just to get that client.

Products – Creating products from your book is an easy and lucrative way to generate more money. Make a video about the book content or just expand on some of the concepts or chapters in the book. Have the audio track lifted and transcribed. You then have a video, audio and written product.

A membership site is one of the easiest products you can create and sell for $47 - $97 a month. For those not sure how to go about that I suggest they write 12 chapters to their book (and a 13th bonus chapter to be used as a give away on your website). Each chapter should be a lead magnet in its own right – a title that has the reader thinking "yeah I need to know that – I would buy the book just to learn that". There is only so much you can write in a book, especially a 150 page book, so you could expand on each of those chapters in your weekly eclass. 13 chapters, divide each chapter into 4 parts and expand on them, gives you 52 weeks of eclasses - you've just created a years worth of content!

Advertise in your book any products or services you want to sell – even if you haven't created them yet. That will show you exactly what demand there is for that product or service. If there isn't any demand, then you have not wasted time and resources creating it. If the demand is high, take the people's contact details and let them know they are on a waiting list and create that *in demand* product for a hungry market.

One of our authorpreneurs, Andrew Verity, ran a registered training organisation at the Kinesiology Institute where they do muscle testing and conduct training courses about it. Literally after his book *The Efficient CEO Brain* was published, it was suggested he offer a different type of training program, a high-end program, based on the credibility the book would generate. To see what demand there would be for it, he announced it before he created it by sending out an email and that one email netted him over $180,000 that he never thought was possible.

That built his confidence in what he was doing and led to gaining new, high paying clients. He's been able to increase his prices massively, all from the credibility that book brought him. He just took some of the knowledge he had and put it in a book and by putting it out there, everything changed in his business life.

If you think the examples of products I have listed here are all too hard for you to create, just start by thinking of things you could do relatively easily to begin with. Can you Joint Venture with someone else who already has some of the products or services you would like to offer? You could sell those complementary items to your customers and receive up to 50% of the profits.

Can you package someone else's goods under your brand through a licensing agreement? This is known as white label products. Someone else creates them and they just put your brand label on it. You pay a price for it, add a mark up, sell it as your own and pocket the difference.

If that sounds like a foreign concept just realise many health supplement manufacturers do exactly that. The one factory produces the supplements, then applies different company labels to the bottles (or in many cases entire new bottles are supplied) and so the exact same product goes out under many different brands. Same thing happens with Aspirin and so many other products, like the herbal tea range I mentioned in a previous chapter.

Then when you do eventually create your own products, start thinking the other way round and look at licensing those goods or services to someone else. Create something that you could Joint Venture partner with someone and have them sell your new stuff and promote your brand.

I wrote in the previous chapter about use of AI tools not being suitable for creating your Authority Influencer Marketing book but being perfect for helping create course, short books, eclasses and more. The mechanics of how to do that are outside the scope of this book but some simple research will reveal ways you can use simple tools like ChatGPT to create so much product content for you in just a few hours.

Once you accept what is possible, you start thinking differently and these sort of opportunities, that you've never considered before, become obvious, abundant and easily accessible.

Selling these products leads to more -

Profits – The idea is to build multiple streams of income from your book. You have the products themselves as one stream. You could be looking at professional speaking gigs from your new positioning as another stream. Of course you should always be considering The Game Behind The Game, what is all this ultimately working towards? Is it to allow you to grow your business and earn extra money that way? Is it to allow you to charge more than you are now and be able to work less? Is it to create far more value in your business so that you can sell it at a much higher price? Is it to allow you to gain more franchisees or have people pay more to own a franchise? Are you considering licensing deals?

Just keep in mind that the profit your book makes you shouldn't be made from sales of the book itself. That is a traditional way of thinking that has no place in Entrepreneurial Publishing. Authorpreneurs are actually happy giving their books away for free, knowing how much money the products and services advertised in them will bring them, and how much extra customers that will bring them, and knowing how the book will help them achieve their Game Behind The Game.

So in summary –
Your book is THE lead generator. It's helping your business, as if it is on steroids.

It positions you as the authority, gives you all this credibility and builds immediate trust, so that you get all this extra business.

After you start the initial marketing for your book, it can attract massive free media and promote your brand and message in a way you never could before.

It helps you advertise and develop new products and test the market for them first.
This brings in far greater profits and you can do much more if you use your book to develop a Game Behind The Game.

Ultimately, your book gives you access to other influencers and is the perfect way to share your message, build your brand, support a charity or make a massive difference to many others, all while creating your own legacy.

How do I know all this works? My company has run live in person workshops for over 15 years, that cover everything in this book in far greater depth and has helped thousands of people. We have personally worked one on one with hundreds and hundreds of authors to generate phenomenal results, just some of which have been covered in this book. We have bestselling authors all around the world. We are known for creating the highest number of genuine Bestselling Authors. We have the proven strategies, the resources and all the contacts in the industry to make this happen time and again.

There are very few industries that we haven't published a book for or that we haven't worked with somebody in, to create a huge success for them. You can do this as well.

All the author examples given in this book are completely verifiable. They were printed and distributed by the Entrepreneurial Publisher, Global Publishing Group. You can find a full list of those authors and their books at **www.GlobalPublishingGroup.com.au**

I've included their real life examples in this book because they are everyday people - just like you, just like me - but by using a book to build authority or celebrity status, it catapulted their brand and business and opened up all these opportunities that they never even knew were there. You need to think outside the box and to know that this is possible for you.

It is important at this point to understand why I wrote this book and how you can best benefit from it.

I had a conversation with Konrad Bobilak who wrote *Australian Property Finance Made Simple* discussed in Chapter 6 and he told me he wrote that book because he was sick of seeing 22 year old, self appointed 'authorities' on social media, stating how to purchase property and obtain finance, when they had no idea what they were talking about.

Those people had their parents help fund the deposit for their first house. Because times were good, equity increased quickly and they used that as a deposit on another house and then eventually another. So with 3 or 4 houses behind them in a few years, these people were telling others how clever they were and how they could teach people to do the same. However, they were teaching a system that only worked at that particular time, not something that could withstand large interest rate rises or property values decreasing or any other number of variables, that they had not encountered or were even aware of.

Konrad on the other hand, over 30 years, had seen 3 complete economic cycles from the 'recession we had to have', to the downturn at the beginning of this century, to the Global Financial Crisis and the surprise times created by the COVID epidemic years. He had a solid background in finance, lending and real estate with National Australia Bank over 20 years. So he was dumbfounded watching the following the 22 year old amateurs were amassing, and how damaging the information they provided could be in the long run.

I'm now seeing more and more of the same sort of thing appear on social media in the book writing or book publishing space. There are a lot of people claiming to be gurus and making all sorts of promises like making anyone a published author within 60 days or 30 days or 14 days. There are people claiming they can help you produce an ebook in 7 days or people who will take the content you already have online and turn that into an ebook for you. Others are trying to sell people into AI programs that will write an ebook for them, in a fashion.

I mention those things here for you to be wary of. If you're looking at investing in real estate, you will learn so much from Konrad, and so little from the 22 year old on YouTube. If you are looking at positioning yourself as an expert, build trust and dominate in your industry, then you will learn more from this book and the 15 years of incredible results our company has generated for so many other business owners, then you will from the online armchair 'experts' making claims that ultimately just don't deliver.

Sure they might be able to help get you a finished product but they don't have the experience, longevity, understanding, techniques or contacts in the industry to do it the way covered here, and get the desired results you need **and most importantly get your book distributed, into bookstores and many other platforms**. Anyone can produce a book, very few can produce a best selling and best positioning book – yet that is what we do constantly.

Very few companies, even established publishing houses will offer you distribution. Global Publishing do for the authors they take on, because without getting your book out to the masses, what point was there in creating it in the first place?

How you decide to produce your book and get it to the masses is entirely your choice. It is important however to remember some key points that will make all the difference between massive success and disappointing mediocrity. I know as I have seen this so many times.

I want you to take the time and decide exactly what it is you are trying to achieve. Because if you want to position yourself as a go-to authority and stand out from all competition, if you want to generate free media and PR on a scale you hadn't thought possible, and if you want to build massive trust and have ideal customers or clients come seek you out, then your book has to be done the ways described in this book.

Don't skip a step or two. Don't try taking shortcuts to get something mediocre produced quicker. It won't generate the same results. Don't go down a purely ebook path or look at only online sales of your book.

Done properly, your book is the ultimate lead generation tool. The best form of marketing that you can have working for you, for literally years and years. So take the time to get it right and make it work for you.

The information contained in this book is more than enough for you to follow and succeed. I have given as much here as I possibly can to ensure your best success. I am however, well aware that some people want assistance creating their book and getting it to market. Having the proper guidance and support and a proven system to follow ensures you avoid costly mistakes in time and money along the way and get a better product, sooner. I can help those who want that assistance. More about that at the end of the next chapter.

CHAPTER ELEVEN

Getting it out to the Masses

Good Marketing makes the company employees feel good. Great Marketing makes the customer feel Good.

A book is the best way to market you and your business. Done properly it is truly Great Marketing.

Andrew Carter

CHAPTER ELEVEN

Getting it out to the Masses

In order to produce your physical book and get it out there, it has to be published and distributed. Those are the two areas where most authorpreneurs come unstuck. There only ever use to be two options, both of which had major drawbacks but there is a third option designed especially for Authority and Influencer Marketing. This chapter covers all three options in detail.

Traditional Publishing

This is what everyone is familiar with. Anytime you walk into a book store, the majority of books you are looking at are published by traditional publishers. Those publishers are just that – traditional thinking. They have been doing books the same way for centuries. Sure, the technology has changed and the way books are typeset, printed and even distributed has improved over time, but the mentality behind the book as a product has not.

There are a large number of rules around what a traditional publisher will allow in a book and how they produce all the elements that make up the book for it to be sold in book stores. These are not rules you can find listed. These are just the way things have always been done in the traditional publishing world and taught to those who work in it.

For those not associated with the industry, the general perception of the process is –

You write the manuscript, you send it to a publisher, they accept it, do all the work, publish and distribute it and you just sit back and watch the money roll in. **Though that is the perception, it most certainly is <u>not</u> the reality.**

Once you send a manuscript to a publisher, they might take it on. However, they receive far more works than they can ever publish, so they are incredibly selective and send out far more rejection letters / emails, than they do ones of acceptance. Traditional publishers prefer established or proven authors to reduce their workload and risks.

If your work was accepted, you need to know that the publisher has complete say over the entire design and layout of your book, including the cover. You have no input into the process at all. A great example of how problematic this can be was when *The Mars & Venus Diet & Exercise Solution*, was distributed by a traditional publisher in Australia. They created their own cover design, which was not good. John Gray wanted them to stick to what had already been proven good for sales in the USA. The publisher refused. As a result, initial book sales here were poor, until the publisher finally acquiesced and went back to the original format.

Traditional publishers do not allow advertising in books. If you have sold advertising space to people and then the book is published and those ads aren't in it, you could find yourself in a lot of trouble.

It usually takes traditional publishers 18 – 24 months from the time your manuscript is accepted, to get your book to market. That is a very long time to wait.

You can expect to be paid about 3% - 5% commission of the cover price of your book and they set the price of the book. So on a book you should expect to sell for $30, they may sell it for under $20 and so you can expect to see between 50 cents and $1.00 per each book sold.

To really rub salt into the wounds, if you want to buy your own book (to promote yourself at speaking gigs or other events) you have to pay the publisher 50% of the retail price!

What most would be authors don't know is that as a first time author you would still be expected to do the initial publicity for your book.

Self-Publishing
It is because the drawbacks of going with a traditional publisher are so many, for the very little benefit of maybe getting a book out there, that many authors turned to self-publishing. With the increase in technology and resources available at large commercial printers and Office Works type facilities, this has become far easier for people to do and the end result looks far more professional now than was possible even just 10 years ago.

The benefits of self-publishing are many. First and foremost you make far more money per book, somewhere between $3 - $23 a book on a book that sells for $30. However, remember the real money to be made from your book shouldn't be coming from the sales of your book.

You can get it printed and into the hands of readers much faster than traditional publishers, on average around 16 weeks versus almost 2 years. Most importantly you keep full control over every aspect of the design and look of your book. You do the cover the way you want, typeset the way you want and add in any advertising you want.

However, those benefits do come at a price.

You have to design, proofread, layout and print your book to the international publishing standards and arrange barcodes and ISBN numbers and ensure they are placed in the correct locations on your book. This is not as easy as it may initially seem. As I wrote at the beginning of this chapter, the rules around all this are not something you can find easily, even on the internet. Afterall, why would traditional publishers want to make it easy for self-publishers?

As a self-publisher you have to request international library cataloguing numbers and register with the national libraries and lodge a sample book and ensure you meet all the national legal requirements around publishing that book.

To make it economically viable, you need to print in large numbers to get the cost per book as low as possible. If you then have difficulty finding enough people to sell to, you end up holding and having to store all your stock and then when able, package, ship and deliver to your customers.

The worst part about self-publishing is that book distributors won't deal with you.

Book distributors only want to deal with book publishers. So to get your book into a book store, you need to approach each store directly. However, the book stores don't want to deal with hundreds of different authors and place orders with each of them. That's why they use distributors – the same distributors who won't touch your book because it is self-published.

Simply put, book stores generally only deal with distributors and recognised publishers.

Although it seems a bit snobbish, many book buyers just don't like self-published books! This is in large part simply because the look and more importantly the entire layout of most self-published books simply isn't up to the standard of professionally published books. They look like self-published books OR somehow just don't look quite professional. Remember Authority and Professionalism go hand in hand. **People won't see you as professional if your book doesn't look professional.**

Just because your book may look professional to your or your friends, doesn't mean it does to others or to the industry at large. As was explained to me by someone working for the largest distributor in Australia, just by looking at the back cover, yet alone the binding or the typesetting of the text, he can tell instantly if a book has been self published, regardless of what standard the author thought it was.

I have had people approach me with self published books that they assure me are identical to similar books that have been completed with a professional publisher and found in book stores and so I should distribute them. When I look at the book, I can instantly see the issues with it. Often, even when I point those out to the author, they just can't see the difference. So again, just because it's not obvious to you, your friends or your family, doesn't mean it isn't obvious to those in the industry or to the reader you are trying to attract.

Entrepreneurial publishing – the best of all worlds.

The limitations of self-publishing and traditional publishing are just way too high for anyone looking to publish a book for their own Authority and Influencer Marketing. There had to be a way to bring together the best of both but without any of the limitations.

That is how Global Publishing Group was created. **The first true Entrepreneurial Publisher that allowed entrepreneurs to produce the books the way they needed to**. *Books that provided great information but also allowed the author to promote themselves, their products or services and those of others, whilst driving traffic to a website to build a list and ultimately to work on The Game Behind The Game.*

Global Publishing Group makes it easy and more profitable for you. It gets you published and recognised. Distributors deal with us as we are a recognised and respected publisher with more than 16 years in the industry, so your book can go into book stores and many other platforms. We have over 50,000 different sales outlets worldwide.

So does Authoritative Marketing and Entrepreneurial Publishing only work for businesses?

Not at all! Any industry, hobby, organisation or even life experience can be completed under the Authority Marketing system and generate exactly the same high-end results. Just some of the non-business books we have published which have made the authors the experts in their field and in many cases made them a lot of money from their interests, are -

Yachting

cook books

better relationships

learn how to paint

make money from art

learn how to play the keyboard

Angels

better sex

Basketball for beginners

Beat PTSD

coping with suicide

books on marriage

books on moving out of home

dealing with autism

Elizabeth Island

Kangaroo Island

Coping with Alzheimer's

first time mum at 50

fitness books

dating books

raising kids

beating depression

dealing with dyslexia

Motorcycling adventures

Colic relief

weight loss

Horsemanship

Self help and self healing

If you are passionate about it, you can write a book about it. If you use the methods described in this book, you can make money from it, by using the entrepreneurial publisher.

So in summary –

Traditional Publishers -
Prefer well known or established proven authors.
They have all the say in your design.
You can't advertise or market in your book.
You have to purchase your own book back from them at 50% off retail.
They take 18-24 months to bring your book to market.
They pay you 3% - 5% of the cover price that they set (50c - $1.00 on a $20 book).

They handle all distribution and book store orders and sales.

May lock you into a contract where all your future books are to be published by them.

You will still be responsible for marketing your book.

Self-Publishing

Make more money ($3 - $23 a book on a $30 book)

More flexibility to sell your books into other markets – no restrictions

Get to the printers sooner (16 weeks versus 2 years)

Keep control of your work and designs

You can market and advertise in your own book

However -

You have to design, proof read, layout arrange barcodes and ISBN numbers and print your book to the international publishing standards, not as easy as it may initially seem.

You have to request international library cataloguing numbers and register with the national libraries and lodge a sample book. You must meet all legal obligations.

You have to hold and warehouse all your stock.

You have to package, ship and deliver to your individual customers.

Being self-published most book distributors won't deal with you and it is unlikely you will get your book into book stores, severely limiting the reach and exposure and ultimately the credibility your book and you will receive.

Entrepreneurial Publishing –

Literally gives you the best of both worlds. Allows you all the benefits of self-publishing but does so in a professional manner and includes Distribution which is the most difficult aspect of publishing. This has your book distributed to far more outlets nationally and internationally through the Entrepreneurial Publishers strong association with industry distributors. Entrepreneurial publishing has been expertly designed to allow you to advertise in your book, build and promote back end products and use your book as a tool to deliberately work towards your Game Behind The Game.

Again, regardless of what subject you decide to write about, your book will get you -
access to other influencers and is the perfect way to share your message, build your brand, support a charity or make a massive difference to many others, all while creating your own legacy.

Additional points to consider.

The success for authors using *the* Entrepreneurial Publisher, Global Publishing Group, comes from us being master marketers first and foremost who have transferred that skill into books to use them as the ultimate marketing tool. We understand the workings of the human mind from a marketing perspective. We have extensive business and marketing backgrounds.

We have done the research and know that you only have 7 seconds to capture someone's attention with the design of the front cover of your book. Anyone can come up with a title for a book but we know how to come up with an attention grabbing title, as best selling title, that will attract the ideal client for you.

People pick up a book based on the front cover and most importantly the title. If it has interested them enough, they turn over to the back cover and then you have 14 seconds in which to convince them to buy.

Now there are plenty of graphic artists, traditional publishers, armchair 'experts' on social media and want-to-be publishers who will tell you they can design a great looking cover for you for a fee. So what?! A great looking cover is not enough. For what you want to achieve, you need a cover that sells - and there are very few people who actually know how to produce that.

Our rear covers are designed like a sales letter, to grab attention, keep people reading and close the sale inside that 14 second window. There is a science behind it. One we have refined over time and it works consistently well. This remains something I am yet to see other publishers do and is one of the main reasons books with us tend to stand out so well ahead of any competitors in the same space.

What you have read in this book has proved to be a winning formula for literally thousands of authors over the last 15 years and continues to be the best method for success. Some of those authors are very high profile and others are just regular business owners who as a result really stood out and dominated in their field, making them far more money in their business or from their hobby, than they ever expected.

If you want to position yourself as the go-to expert, follow the advice in this book. Do it properly and succeed. You will need to get your book published. You will need to sign a distribution deal as you do need to get your books into book stores for the credibility and added exposure that brings – even if that in itself may not generate the most sales, that's not the point. This is about generating free media and positioning you.

For those who need assistance or would like to fast track their journey and have all the difficult aspects taken care of for them - and have a genuine publishing deal with World Wide Distribution, I do offer a Fast Track Authors Program, by application only. This program has helped position literally hundreds of authors as the go-to trusted authority. The program is a complete online membership program with absolutely all the resources you need to create a book that will allow you to dominate in your industry.

Most importantly it allows you to work with me and my dedicated team who give you unlimited ongoing support and assistance. We run special workshops to hone your concept, build your business (back end products and Game Behind The Game), accelerate the entire process and provide the ultimate marketing weekend to show you how to break through all the clutter and promote you, your book and your business better than anyone else is doing! And of course making you money before your book is even printed and even pre selling thousands of copies.

So how quickly can YOU actually complete a book?
You take the time you need to get the right product for you. You won't be rushed. If you need it done fast, following our fast track system and working with my team, it can literally be created in just 2 weeks! That's all the content done by you, all legal obligations, cover design, ISBN, barcode etc, done by us - all in just 2 weeks.

One author who did that was Karen Scott who actually typed the manuscript rather than record and transcribe it - and she did so with fractured vertebrae in her neck, so she had a constant headache the entire time. She had a deadline she wanted to meet, so did the work on the content and Global Publishing Group took care of everything else to ensure everything was completed in the required time. This is what is possible with the correct system and support.

And of course the biggest advantage is that we have national and international distribution for our authors. Writing a book is one thing but doesn't mean much unless you get it out to the masses.

If you'd like to learn more about the easiest way to writing a book and find out more about Entrepreneurial Publishing and how it can work for you, go to **www.MarketingInfluencer.com.au** and book a time for a call to discuss.

CHAPTER TWELVE

Accelerated Learning

There is no passion to be found playing small—in settling for a life that is less than the one you are capable of living.

Nelson Mandela

CHAPTER TWELVE

Accelerated Learning

> *You are your greatest asset. Put your time, money and effort into training, grooming and encouraging your greatest asset.*
>
> **Tom Hopkins**

It was the great copywriter Ted Nicholas who said –

The three best ways to learn things are to invest in:
- *Great books for you are exposed to the synthesis of the world's best minds.*
- *Great seminars given by those rare practitioners who practice what they preach.*
- *Travel, as meeting and knowing people and visiting new places in different cultures is an irreplaceable education.*

In Chapter 5, I wrote that I had invested heavily in seminars and mentors and attribute my success to that. Maybe I would have still made it on my own but I doubt it. Even if I could have, I know it would have taken a lot longer as I wouldn't have been shown the quickest and easiest way to massive success.

I always suggest to others that the greatest investment you can ever make is in yourself. Like Ted said, you should read great books, you should go to seminars and attend the right courses. It is one of the best investments you can make and it certainly was the case for me. Don't let your subconscious project fear and doubt about trying something new. Travel and try new things, learn from and enjoy the experiences and grow as a result of them.

Never think you are too old to do anything because another of our authors, Kawena Gordon, wrote her first book *Happiness is Just a Breath Away* at 81 years old. She wrote her second book at age 89! She loved it as it transformed her life. She was giving tours in her 90's to people at bookstores and in old age homes. She was inspiring people in their 70's to live longer and do more. So never think that you're too old.

Never think you are too young. Emily Shai wrote the *5 Steps to a Perfect Sleepover* at just 11 years of age and has had phenomenal success, selling over tens of thousands of dollars worth of books! She now inspires and educates other kids to write a book.

Far too many people use expense as the reason they won't try new things that will ultimately benefit them. Unfortunately, we know the cost of everything but the value of nothing. I guess that's where I've been truly lucky. I understand the value of something over the long term. If it is going to help me grow and be more successful, I find a way to pay for it. I've taken loans to help me pay for things that generate more money. I've never done that for things that don't, even though that's what most people do (and maybe a large part of why they're not successful?)

The truly successful understand the difference between good debt and bad debt. Good debt is borrowing to invest in appreciating assets, anything that will help you grow your wealth like property, certain stocks, and your education. Bad debt is borrowing money to purchase depreciating items like most cars, boats, large TV's, furniture, whitegoods etc.

I attend a lot of seminars, not just to learn from the experts but to actually spend time with smarter people, people who have been there, done it and actually achieved what I want to achieve. By spending time with those people, you can learn so much and fast track your success because they've made the mistakes before and learnt from them, thereby finding the best ways to succeed.

Too many people don't want to try something new for fear of making mistakes. Mistakes are normal. They are a natural part of learning.

How many mistakes did you make learning to walk, or later in life learning to drive a car? Mistakes never stopped you then did they, so why would you feel it is so debilitating now?

I've made plenty of mistakes. In fact I believe I've made more mistakes than anyone I've ever met – but that's because I've tried more things than anyone I've ever met. Making mistakes and learning from them is what makes us successful. So never think of your mistakes as failure, for they are an essential step in your ultimate achievements and success.

That is why I am so excited to share all this with you. I know that if you apply the strategies I've shared with you in these pages, you will absolutely transform the success of your business. Remember though that knowledge on its own is not power. Only knowledge *put into practice* is power. **Simply reading this book is not enough. <u>You need to take action.</u>**

Depending on where you are in your business right now you may have lots of reasons not to take immediate action. When you first start out in business or when your business is growing, your attention gets pulled in lots of different directions, you end up wearing multiple hats. You're wearing the hat of the salesman, you're wearing the hat of the receptionist, you're wearing the hat of the bookkeeper, the IT guy, the marketer, maybe even the cleaner, and many others, and that can be really stressful, right? You run from one task to the other trying to keep it all going.

However, the reality is the true success of your business is based totally on the ability for you to attract and drive targeted traffic that converts both online and offline into your business.

That is the success of your business. Without you being able to direct that traffic to your business, it doesn't matter what type of business you're in, your business is not going to succeed. You need to implement the strategies covered in these pages, to position yourself as that credible authority so that you can attract that traffic and enjoy the benefits of being successful.

Think about this. If all publishing a book does is help you grow your brand and give you more customers that already want to buy your product or service, would it be worth it?

If all that did was actually gave you the lifestyle that you've always dreamed about, and gave you the resources and the time so you can have more freedom, more flexibility more time off, would it be worth it?

Would it be worth taking the time to invest in yourself to actually put this in place?

If the answer to any one of those questions is 'yes' then you owe it to yourself to have a book published and see these benefits first hand. Even if you are time poor, we can help. You can become that authority, that go-to expert, by joining like minded people and write a bestselling book. We'll show you step by step how to do that.

In this book I can only cover a small but important part of the real success being a published author can create for you.

If this is all new to you, yet you can clearly see the benefit to produce the ultimate marketing tool (your book) but just aren't ready yet, then you will benefit massively by attending our live event.

There is so much more to being truly successful that I share in a unique live interactive workshop. I show you the full workings and insider secrets in complete detail. I even have previous authors on stage talking about their achievements, so you can question them about the process and their success.

This unique event is not a multi speaker pitch fest, nor is it just a teaser where I only give you enough whet your appetite. I will give you all the information you need. That said, this event is not me talking straight for three days. This is an interactive workshop where you actually work on your book, in real time with real feedback and guidance along the way. Even if you have no idea what you would write a book about, we will work with you to develop that. You'd be surprised how many people attend knowing they need to write a book but not what it will be about – and leave pleasantly surprised and well on their way to completing a book!

You will leave the workshop with your Title and Subtitle done and tested, the front and rear cover design complete and the idea for the chapters of your book done, so that the skeleton of the book (the hardest part) is already completed and you just need to flesh it out, easily done using the techniques in this book, and covered in depth at the workshop.

We cover truly innovative and creative ways to market your book far more effectively than anyone else is doing, again positioning you far above any competition.

To find out more go to www.BestSellerEvent.com

This will be one of the most exciting things you do in your career and a game changer for your business. That's why I'm so passionate about sharing it with others, because once you know this and what happens from it you will be so grateful that you did this.

I offer a full 100% money back guarantee for the entire event. It is such a small outlay for what you are going to get out of it and I can offer that guarantee as you will get so, so much more than you expected.

Again, visit www.BestSellerEvent.com to find out more.

If however you understand the power of this in your business and need to act now, and you are interested in the Fast Track Authors Program, then you should BOOK A CALL now. Simply contact **admin@GlobalPublishingGroup.com.au** to organise the best day and time for one of our team specialists to call you and discuss your business and needs.

Thank you and I look forward to seeing you at our next event and on the bestselling list.

GLOSSARY

Ascension model – see *value ladder*

Authority Influencer Marketing - the process by which you establish yourself as an expert in your industry. If people perceive you as a leader in a certain field, they are far more likely to purchase your products, services and advice and in fact pay more for it.

Authorpreneur – an entrepreneur who has used a book for Authority Marketing and has
created in that a back end and maybe even a *Game Behind the Game*.

Back end (products or sales) - all the additional products that a customer will buy from you over the time that they remain your customer. Because you know what they've already bought from you, you should have a good idea of other things your customers would likely buy.

Bestseller – A badge of honour bestowed upon a book for selling so many thousands (number varies from country to country). Not to be confused with Amazon 'bestseller' which varies continuously and has no kudos or status in the publishing world.

Entrepreneurial publishing – The only form of publishing that allows true Authority Marketing for entrepreneurs to achieve their desired aims in a book. It takes the best of Traditional publishing and self-publishing without any of the limitations.

Game Behind the Game – is the ultimate reason to publish a book. It is what you ultimately want to achieve in business that is possible through the use of a book but is far larger than the sales of the book or some products you might sell from it.

Halo effect – When you position yourself alongside or are seen with more successful people, it gives one similar status and credibility by association.

'How to' book – Informative Non Fiction book detailing how to become successful in a particular area or on a certain topic.

'Me too' business – just another business doing the same thing as every other type of business, offering the same products and services in the same way, usually at the same price with no differentiation from any other business, being left awash in a sea of mediocrity.

Value Ladder – model of increasing costs for goods or services to sell to customers wanting more from you.

RESOURCES
SECTION

Listed in here are resources you can use to best help you and your business. The companies listed are the ones I have used personally and are the experts in their field.

The quickest way to success is to use the skills of others, those that can bring you the best results. They are covered in the following pages and I personally recommend each of them.

Incredible FREE Bonus Offer just for purchasing this book

This is my way of rewarding the action takers. Many people have access to the same opportunities, yet few actually act on them. You have taken action by purchasing this book. Your business will succeed in a massive way if you continue to take action and apply what you learn in this book.

To encourage you to continue to take action at every stage I want you to have access to these incredibly helpful gifts **worth over $400 dollars**, all free of charge.

By using the QR code below (or visiting the website) you will get access to –

- A unique one off, live on stage, private video presentation by the man who wrote the forward for this book and applied the principles within to create a business paying him $1 million a year. In that 45 minutes he will break down step by step the exact process he uses and show you how you can do the same in your business.

- A digital download copy of my first two business books, written a long time ago but updated and still completely relevant today. One of those books was used as a coursebook and essential reading for the Advertising and Marketing course at the University of Canberra.

- Completely free (and obligation free) one on one introductory meeting (online or on phone) with five of the top professional organisations that can help you generate far more money in your business.

- Special, heavily discounted price for intensive live in person workshop to truly transform your business.

Just scan this QR code or go to
www.MarketingInfluencer.com.au

Are you ready to quickly and easily create YOUR own Authority Marketing book?

The easiest way to do it is the same way hundreds of authors including the ones listed in this book have done it, though the Fast Track Bestseller system.

This program includes absolutely everything you need to complete your book in the shortest time and have access to all the resources to make your book generate money before it is published and become a bestselling book once it is published.

To learn more go to – **www.MarketingInfluencer.com.au**

Image for representative purposes only.
Content is now available completely online.

Useful websites and online tools

Otter.ai
speech to text transcription application using artificial intelligence and machine learning. Its software shows captions for live speakers, and generates written transcriptions of the speeches.

Obviously there are other versions of speech to text transcription all making claims that seem doubtful. Few have a free trial version like Otter and that's why I recommend you try this one first.

Copycreator.com
Say Goodbye to Writer's Block! Pick a generator, type in a couple of keywords, and let the magic happen! You'll never be staring at a blank page again!

Searchie.io
Searchie is a web-based software platform that allows you to create, manage, and sell your content all in one place. Designed with content creators in mind,

ChatGPT.com / ChatAI.com
AI Creation service that can help quickly and easily generate a lot of content. Be wary of its use. It will not personalise a story for you and that's the important bit that people will connect with. Can be extremely use for some research and for creating content for back end products.

Freelance sites
Sites to outsource everything from transcription services to website building, logo creation, content creation - pretty much anything you can think of.

fivver.com   freelancer.com   upwork.com   guru.com

Scale Like Crazy with YouTube Ads!

If you're looking to stand out from your competitors and stop being the best-kept secret, then look no further than YouTube Advertising. In today's digital age, where attention is the ultimate currency, YouTube has emerged as the premier platform for businesses to showcase their brand, reach their target audience, and skyrocket their growth.

Titan Marketer, understand the immense power of YouTube marketing and have honed their expertise to help businesses unlock their full potential. As the leading agency in the industry, Titan offer unmatched expertise, experience, and strategies to make sure your business stands out and achieves incredible success.

What sets Titan Marketing apart from the competition? It is their unique approach to YouTube advertising. They don't just create generic campaigns; they craft compelling and personalised content that resonates with your audience, drives engagement, and converts viewers into loyal customers.

Partnering with Titan Marketer will transform your business. They provide comprehensive services that cover every aspect of YouTube advertising, including planning campaigns, producing videos, optimizing channels, targeting specific audiences, and tracking performance. Their goal is not only to help you reach a wider audience but also to maximize your return on investment and deliver tangible results.

YouTube is the best opportunity for your business to break free from obscurity and make a lasting impact. Shockingly, only 8% of advertisers are tapping into the vast potential of YouTube ads to grow their businesses. It is the bluest ocean to market your business in.

If you are spending at least $2,000 monthly or more on digital advertising, visit Titanmarketer.com and book a 45-minute YouTube strategy session and see how they can help you achieve remarkable results using YouTube Ads. They will create a marketing strategy that sets you apart and propels your business towards unparalleled success.

www.titanmarketer.com

Your Business Needs Professional Writing, Advertising and Marketing

<u>Not all agencies are the same.</u> You need someone that understands your needs and can deliver results.

If You want all the advantages of an advertising agency, without any of the extra costs, then contact the professional we have always used.

Who
David Foxx is a career writer with over 30 years' professional experience in advertising, marketing, customer loyalty and communications. He has worked for leading advertising agencies and for numerous leading brands including Telstra, Qantas, Subaru, Makita, Adobe, Microsoft, Westpac, Nestle, Global Publishing Group and many, many more. He has considerable knowledge of the finance, insurance, IT, telecoms, FMCG and agriculture sectors.

What
Sharpen your branding and advertising.
Build strong, long-lasting customer relationships.
Integrate effective words with elegant design.
Deploy more impactful collateral, campaigns and customer communications.
Get expert writing advice, to help you complete an even better best-seller.

Why
Writing is much more than typing words and having AI check the grammar. It's the art of integrating language with strategy, structure, placement and design.

In the same way a jeweller works with diamonds, a good writer will use cut-through, clarity, combination and context to achieve a truly brilliant result.

That's why experience matters so much.

So let's take your business to the next level of strategic thinking and carefully crafted messaging.

No middle-men. No agency overheads. You just deal directly with the talent.

How
Start the conversation via email:
foxx@getfoxx.com.au

Availability is limited, but if you are serious about giving your business a truly premiere public profile, then contact Foxx.

How Much is YOUR Accountant costing YOUR Business?

Not all accountants are the same and the right one can save you tens or even hundreds of thousands of dollars a year!

I know, I've had multiple accountants over the last 20 years and finally found the one who takes care of my needs, professionally and personally.

You need an accountant who is proactive, who works at tax minimisation strategies specific to your situation. Someone who can help plan your business and personal finances and strategy, to avoid nasty surprises or tax bills in the future. Someone who is prepared to go the extra mile for you.

These days it doesn't matter where you live, geographic location is no longer a limitation. You don't need a local accountant, you just need the best accountant available.

Henry Williams has proved to be the most professional and most personable I have had the pleasure of dealing with in the last 35 years and I can't recommend him or his service highly enough, for anyone serious about improving their business and personal financial situation.

Contact him and let him know you read about him here, to book a FREE one on one session with him to find out how he can best help you.

H N Williams Pty Ltd
Accounting and Taxation

CHARTERED ACCOUNTANTS™
AUSTRALIA • NEW ZEALAND

Email: henry@hnwilliams.com.au
Phone: 07 32408420

UNLOCK THE POWER OF META ADVERTISING

Meta (which includes Facebook, Instagram, WhatsApp and Messenger) is the largest social media platform in the world, with more than half the world's population using one of its apps, so if a business owner wants to stand out, get more leads and make more sales, it makes sense to be advertising on this channel, yet most business owners shy away from dipping their toe in the Metaverse and investing money on ads!

Why is that? Because most business owners find it way too overwhelming, time-consuming and expensive to try and get results and a return on investment!

That's where Kerry Fitzgibbon and her digital team of ads angels come in, with over 13 years hands-on working with clients all around the world, helping them master and make money from Facebook (now Meta) ads.

Kerry has a proven system that can quickly and cheaply build a targeted list that is ready to buy.. with this system she has

- Added whole new income streams to businesses in under 7-days
- Bult warm, ready-to-buy lists of ideal clients for just a few cents per lead
- Helped businesses increase revenue many-fold in under a month
- Launched brand new businesses (concept to cash) in just 2 weeks
- And more….

This passionate, tenacious, and determined woman has run over 60 marathons, including running 12 Ultra-Marathons (50KM/ 31.6 miles) in 12 consecutive days to raise money charity. She is also the proud owner of "Marathon Girl®", an international sportswear brand with the tag-line "Never mess with a woman who runs 42.2km or 26.2 Miles just for fun".

Think of it like this… if this gal has the willpower to run marathons, then she's got enough grit, determination, and perseverance to tackle just about anything including helping business owners make money from Meta Ads. And let's not forget her massive goal-setting abilities – this is the kind of person you want on your marketing team!

To find out how you can get Kerry and her team to help you master meta and make more money with paid advertising – scan the QR code and see for yourself what she can do for you!

When and Why Do You Need a Lawyer for You and Your Business?

In the dynamic and highly competitive world of business, entrepreneurs face numerous challenges and complexities that demand expert guidance. A competent and experienced lawyer becomes a vital ally for any thriving business. From providing legal advice to ensuring compliance with regulations, Lawyers play a vital role in safeguarding business interests and fostering growth.

Not all lawyers or law firms are the same. I use the ones who best understand my personal and business needs and have the experience to achieve the results in the least possible time and that's why I recommend Cornerstone law offices.

Just some compelling reasons why having a lawyer for your business is of utmost importance:

Legal Compliance:
The legal landscape can be daunting, with businesses subject to a wide array of regulations and laws. A Lawyer can assist in ensuring that the company complies with all applicable rules and regulations, lowering the possibility of fines, penalties, or lawsuits for noncompliance. This may include local, state and federal government particularly if you're looking at buying or selling a business or a commercial entity.

Contracts and Agreements:
Businesses enter into numerous contracts and agreements on a regular basis. These can include partnerships agreements, vendor contracts and independent contractors. Having a Lawyer review and draft these documents ensures that the business or the company's interests are protected, and the terms are fair and favourable. A lot of businesses fail to have these basic but crucial agreements in place and later suffer as a result.

Litigation and Dispute Resolution:
In business, disputes are likely to happen and you must be prepared to handle and defend these. Having a knowledgeable and experienced Lawyer is crucial from the initial stages of such claims. They can represent the company in court, negotiate settlements, or engage in alternative dispute resolution methods to protect and defend the company's interests.

Business Structure and Formation:

When people start a business, the key component which often gets neglected is the emphasis on the Business Structure. A correct business structure and entity can save a lot of time and money when it comes to making changes or when there are potential mergers and acquisitions of the business as it grows over time. Lawyers help entrepreneurs choose the appropriate legal structure for their business, such as sole proprietorship, partnership, or incorporation. The right structure can have significant tax and liability implications as well any government support tender opportunities.

Chasing payments:

One of the biggest causes of business failure is cash flow which often is related to bad debts. If proper initial stages are not followed and documents are not executed in a timely manner, these Debt Collections can be very costly. When polite follow-ups with no response and your patience wears thin, having an effective legal team becomes crucial. A formal letter or a notice from a lawyer dramatically increases the likelihood of a response and payment.

Having a good legal team in your corner is one of the most important parts of the business from the initial start up, through to being established, to when it's time to sell the business or it is in the Merger and Acquisition stage.

I highly recommend speaking with one of the team members at Cornerstone Law Offices to understand the legal road map for your business and to ensure that the core of the business runs smoothly.

Contact them now to book a free 30 minute initial consultation and let them show you how to protect your business or your assets with Cornerstone Law Offices on your side.

Ph - 07 3806 4354
www.cornerstonelawoffices.com.au
An ISO 9001 Quality Accredited Company

ABOUT THE AUTHOR

Andrew Carter, is an Entrepreneur, ex Airline Captain, International Author, Business Mentor, Philanthropist, highly engaging Public Speaker, and CEO of the award-winning Global Publishing Group. He has run three highly successful businesses and founded two Not For Profit organisations. He is a business leader acknowledged for his strategic and marketing intellect and is a recognised authority on aviation, leadership, decision making and business turnaround.

After selling his first business, Andrew started teaching his business success principles to other business owners through his books and personal mentoring, making improvements of literally hundreds of thousands of dollars to their bottom line profits every year. He then took the audacious step of creating the most unique aviation museum in the country which attracted visitors from around the world.

His unique strategies, systems, publishing and marketing tools for wealth creation are empowering thousands around the globe to improve their lives. He is using seminars and workshops to educate and inspire others.

Through his consulting, not for profit entities, books, publishing and business education companies, Andrew has wowed and transformed the lives and businesses of people from all walks of life, including thought leaders, business CEOs, retailers, entrepreneurs and authors.

Andrew as lived and worked all around Australia, in Papua New Guinea, Nauru and Ireland and now resides in Brisbane.

You can find out more about him and the other books he has written at **www.AndrewCarterEvents.com**

Printed in Australia
Ingram Content Group Australia Pty Ltd
AUHW011139070823
381844AU00010B/10

9 781925 370836